S E R I E S

A life-changing encounter
with God's Word from the book of

SONG OF SOLOMON

PROPERTY OF
CHURCH OF CHRIST

A NavPress resource published in alliance
with Tyndale House Publishers, Inc.

NAVPRESS●

NavPress is the publishing ministry of The Navigators, an international Christian organization and leader in personal spiritual development. NavPress is committed to helping people grow spiritually and enjoy lives of meaning and hope through personal and group resources that are biblically rooted, culturally relevant, and highly practical.

For more information, visit www.NavPress.com.

19 18 17 16 15 14
 6   5   4   3   2   1

CONTENTS

HOW TO USE THIS GUIDE

Along with all of the volumes in the LIFECHANGE series of Bible studies, this guide to the Song of Solomon shares common goals:

1. To provide you with a firm foundation of understanding, plus a thirst to return to the Song of Solomon throughout your life.

2. To give you study patterns and skills that help you explore every part of the Bible.

3. To offer you historical background, word definitions, and explanation notes to aid your study.

4. To help you grasp as a whole the message of the Song of Solomon.

5. To teach you how to let God's Word transform you into Christ's image.

As you begin

This guide includes eight lessons that will take you chapter by chapter through all of the Song of Solomon. Each lesson is designed to take from one to two hours of preparation to complete on your own. To benefit most from this time, here's a good way to begin your work on each lesson:

1. Pray for God's help to keep you mentally alert and spiritually sensitive.

2. Read attentively the entire passage mentioned in the lesson's title. (You may want to read the passage from two or more Bible versions—perhaps at least once from a more literal translation such as the New International Version, English Standard Version, New American Standard Bible, or New King James Version and perhaps once more in a paraphrase such as *The Message* or the New Living Translation.) Do your reading in an environment that's as free as possible from distractions. Allow your mind and heart to meditate on the words you encounter—words that are God's personal gift to you and to all His people.

After reading the passage, you're ready to dive into the numbered questions in this guide that make up the main portion of each lesson. Each of these questions is followed by blank space for writing your answers. (This act of writing your answers helps clarify your thinking and stimulates your mental engagement with the passage as well as your later recall.) Use extra paper or a notebook if the space for recording your answers seems too cramped. Continue through the questions in numbered order. If any question seems too difficult or unclear, just skip it and go on to the next.

Each of these questions will typically direct you back to the Song of Solomon to look again at a certain portion of the assigned passage for that lesson. (At this point, be sure to use a more literal Bible translation rather than a paraphrase.)

As you look closer at a passage, it's helpful to approach it in this progression:

Observe. What does the passage actually *say*? Ask God to help you see it clearly. Notice everything that's there.

Interpret. What does the passage *mean*? Ask God to help you understand. And remember that any passage's meaning is fundamentally determined by its *context*. So stay alert to all you'll see about the setting and background of the Song of Solomon, and keep thinking of this book as a whole while you proceed through it chapter by chapter. You'll be progressively building up your insights and familiarity with what it's all about.

Apply. Keep asking yourself, *How does this truth affect my life?* (Pray for God's help as you examine yourself in light of that truth and in light of His purpose for each passage.)

Try to consciously follow all three of these steps as you shape your written answer to each question in the lesson.

The extras

In addition to the regular numbered questions you see in this guide, each lesson also offers several "optional" questions or suggestions that appear in the margins. All of these will appear under one of three headings:

Optional Application. These are suggested options for application. Consider these with prayerful sensitivity to the Lord's guidance.

For Thought and Discussion. Many of these questions address various ethical issues and other biblical principles that lead to a wide range of implications. They tend to be particularly suited for group discussion.

For Further Study. These often include cross-references to other parts of the Bible that shed light on a topic in the lesson, plus questions that delve deeper into the passage.

(For additional help for more effective Bible study, refer to the "Study Aids" section starting on page 145.)

Changing your life

Don't let your study become an exercise in knowledge alone. Treat the passage as *God's* Word and stay in dialogue with Him as you study. Pray, "Lord, what do You want me to notice here?" "Father, why is this true?" "Lord, how does my life measure up to this?"

Let biblical truth sink into your inner convictions so you'll be increasingly able to act on this truth as a natural way of living.

At times, you may want to consider memorizing a certain verse or passage you come across in your study, one that particularly challenges or encourages you. To help with that, write down the words on a card to keep with you and set aside a few minutes each day to think about the passage. Recite it to yourself repeatedly, always thinking about its meaning. Return **to** it as often as you can for a brief review. You'll soon find the words coming to mind spontaneously, and they'll begin to affect your motives and actions.

For group study

Exploring Scripture together in a group is especially valuable for the encouragement, support, and accountability it provides as you seek to apply God's Word to your lives. You can listen jointly for God's guidance, pray for one another, help one another resist temptation, and share the spiritual principles you're learning to put into practice. Together you will affirm that growing in faith, hope, and love is important and that you need one another in the process.

A group of four to ten people allows for the closest understanding of one another and the richest discussions in Bible study, but you can adapt this guide for groups of other sizes. It will suit a wide range of group types, such as home Bible studies, growth groups, and church classes. Both new and mature Christians will benefit from the guide, regardless of their previous experience in Bible study.

Aim for a positive atmosphere of acceptance, honesty, and openness. In your first meeting, explore candidly everyone's expectations and goals for your time together.

A typical schedule for group study is to do one lesson per week, but feel free to split lessons if you want to discuss them more thoroughly. Or omit some questions in a lesson if your preparation or discussion time is limited. (Group members can always study further on their own at a later time.)

When you come together, you probably won't have time to discuss all the questions in the lesson, so it's helpful for the leader to choose ahead of time the ones to be covered thoroughly. This is one of the main responsibilities a group leader typically assumes.

Each lesson in this guide ends with a section called "For the group." It gives advice for that particular lesson on how to focus the discussion, how to apply the lesson to daily life, and so on. Reading each lesson's "For the group" section ahead of time can help the leader be more effective in guiding the group.

You'll get the greatest benefit from your time together if each group member also prepares ahead of time by writing out his or her answers to each question in the lesson. The private reflection and prayer this preparation can stimulate will be especially important in helping group members discern how God wants to apply each lesson to their daily lives.

There are many ways to structure the group meeting, and you may want to vary your routine occasionally to help keep things fresh.

Here are some of the elements you can consider including as you come together for each lesson:

Pray together. It's good to pause for prayer as you begin your time together as well as to incorporate a later more extensive time of prayer for one another, after you've had time to share personal needs and prayer requests (you may want to write these down in a notebook). When you begin with prayer, it's worthwhile and honoring to God to ask especially for His Holy Spirit's guidance of your time together.

Worship. Some groups like to sing together and worship God with prayers of praise.

Review. You may want to take time to discuss what difference the previous week's lesson has made in your lives as well as recall the major emphasis you discovered in the passage for that week.

Read the passage aloud. Once you're ready to focus attention together on the assigned Scripture passage in the week's lesson, read it aloud. (One person could do this, or the reading could be shared.)

Open up for questions. Allow time for group members to mention anything in the passage they may have particular questions about.

Summarize the passage. Have one or two people offer a summary of what the passage says.

Discuss. This will be the heart of your time together and will likely take the biggest portion of your time. Focus on the questions you see as the most important and most helpful. Allow and encourage everyone to be part of the discussion for each question. You may want to take written notes as the discussion proceeds. Ask follow-up questions to sharpen your attention and deepen your understanding of what you discuss. You may want to give special attention to the questions in the margins under the heading "For Thought and Discussion." Remember that sometimes these can be especially good for discussion, but be prepared for widely differing answers and opinions. As you hear one another, keep in mind one another's various backgrounds, personalities, and ways of thinking. You can practice godly discernment without ungodly judgment in your discussion.

Encourage further personal study. You can find more opportunities for exploring this lesson's themes and issues under the heading "For Further Study" in the margins throughout the lesson. You can also pursue some of these together during your group time.

Focus on application. Look especially at the "Optional Application" listed in the margins throughout the lesson. Keep encouraging one another in the continual work of adjusting your lives to the truths God gives in Scripture.

Summarize your discoveries. You may want to read aloud through the passage one last time together, using the opportunity to solidify your understanding and appreciation of it and to clarify how the Lord is speaking to you through it.

Look ahead. Glance together at the headings and questions in the next lesson to see what's coming next.

Give thanks to God. It's good to end your time together by pausing to express gratitude to God for His Word and the work of His Spirit in your minds and hearts during your time together.

Get to know one another better. In early sessions together, you may want to spend time establishing trust, common ground, and a sense of one another's background and what each person hopes to gain from the study. This may help you later with honest discussion about how the Bible applies to each of you. Understanding one another better will make it easier to share about personal applications.

Keep these worthy guidelines in mind throughout your time together:

Let us consider how we may spur one another on toward love and good deeds.

(HEBREWS 10:24)

Carry each other's burdens, and in this way you will fulfill the law of Christ.

(GALATIANS 6:2)

Accept one another, then, just as Christ accepted you, in order to bring praise to God.

(ROMANS 15:7)

THE SONG OF SOLOMON

Lyrics of Love

"Love-lyrics to adorn a wedding celebration"[1] — that's how one commentator describes the Song of Solomon. The book probably isn't meant to be a single unified story. Instead, it's a collection of song lyrics written originally to be sung at wedding feasts. It speaks without embarrassment of the passion between a man and a woman as something to be celebrated. It may also point beyond human love to the love between God and His beloved people.

The book is treasured by both Jews and Christians even though it lacks obvious religious content. Readers are drawn to its poetry that speaks of marriage not as it often is after the fall of Adam, but as it was meant to be. The Old Testament is unflinchingly honest about sex in a fallen world — including polygamy, marital strife, jealousy, rape, and prostitution. Here in the Song of Solomon, however, we glimpse what God intended sex to be: rich in pleasure when pursued faithfully and honorably. Its presence in the Scriptures underscores that God created sexuality with all its passion and physicality as something good. Its message is especially needed in a world blighted by sexual impurity. "God in His wisdom has included in the Canon of Holy Scripture one whole book on this important matter which, in every generation, suffers tragic abuse."[2]

Authorship

Its opening verse names the book "Solomon's Song of Songs." Christians and Jews over the centuries have traditionally seen Solomon as the book's author (see 1 Kings 4:32), though his authorship isn't entirely certain. That opening Hebrew phrase could mean "the Song of Songs by Solomon" (its author) or "the Song of Songs for Solomon" (the king to whom the scribe dedicates the collection). King Solomon, son of David, is mentioned in 1:5; 3:7,9,11; and 8:11-12, but nothing in the book declares clearly that Solomon wrote it. On the other hand, Solomon was well-known as a writer of songs and proverbs, so he could be the author.

11

The characters in the Song

Three main voices alternate in the Song—a young woman, a young man, and, here and there, the united voices of a group of others.

Both bride and groom are probably quite young, perhaps even in their midteens (the typical age for marriage in ancient Israel), and most likely betrothed. In the ancient world, betrothal was binding, unlike a modern engagement. In the early chapters of the Song we can see the betrothed couple taking their first tentative steps to explore their love up until full union in 5:1.

The woman is by far the most prominent person in the lyrics, and her personality and passions are most revealed. She's called a "Shulammite" in 6:13. Some see this as a feminine variation of Solomon's name, or perhaps an indication that she's from the town of Shunem in northern Israel ("Shulammite" deriving from "Shunammite"), or even a variation of "Jerusalemite."

The woman refers to the man as a "king" (1:4,12; 7:5), though she also sees him as a shepherd (see 1:7). In both cases she may be speaking figuratively — he is to her like a king, like a shepherd. The man is shown specifically as the woman's pursuer in 2:4,8-14; 4:8; 5:2,4; and 7:8.

The lyrics address other characters as "daughters of Jerusalem" (1:5), "daughters of Zion" (3:11), or "young women" (1:3); they're seen as friends of the bride. In addition, there are "others" speaking in 8:8-9 who appear to be the woman's brothers. These united plural voices function somewhat like the chorus in an ancient Greek play, commenting on the actions of the bride and groom.

The characters in the Song may or may not have been real individuals, such as Solomon. We're given few details about the two lovers except their thoughts and emotions, but we connect with them because their feelings and actions are typical of men and women in passionate love. They come across as real because their ardor is so deep.

Structure and unity

Most interpreters don't see the Song as a filled-out story with beginning, middle, and end. Most see it as a collection of independent love poems or love songs. Others see tighter unity as a single work, and some have even seen the Song as a kind of drama, at least in part. For most observers today, however, trying to view the Song as a story or drama ultimately proves unsatisfactory. They see it rather as a song cycle or poem cycle. Like most poetry, it is full of repetitions and metaphors.

Because the book's structure is uncertain, Bible versions vary widely in the way they label the various parts. In this guide, as you study through the Song of Solomon, you'll find a few suggested section titles from various sources. Since various Bible translations (through their insertion of headings within the text) approach the book's structure differently, it can help broaden your view of the Song to see these different heading placements.

12

Style

The Song of Solomon is esteemed for its poetic greatness, its "haunting beauty."[3] "To relish reading the Song of Solomon . . . we need to forget about prose literalism and take flight on the wings of the fantastic and poetic imagination. The writer of the Song of Solomon is a poet who pulls out all the stops."[4]

The Song is packed with imagery, some of which seems foreign to us three thousand years after it was written. When we read about doves, fawns, and warriors' shields, we need to ask ourselves, What associations and feelings did this image trigger for its first readers? "Figurative language is not concerned with precision of content. Indeed, imagery both reveals and conceals the object of comparison. To say that the woman's eyes are like doves raises all sorts of questions that are difficult to answer. . . . In what way are her eyes like doves?"[5]

Getting used to the Song's intense use of metaphor becomes easier as we learn to accept the Song on its own terms. We have to avoid imposing on it the standards by which we would judge a modern love song. To assist you in this process, this study differs from what you may have experienced in other LIFECHANGE studies. You will dive deep into the metaphors used throughout the book and reflect on the marital themes communicated through them.

Who is speaking when?

In the Hebrew of the Song of Solomon, there's no indication of where one speaker ends and another begins. Sometimes it's unclear where these transitions occur. To help modern readers with this, many Bible translations have inserted speaker identification headings into the text. Translations vary as to where they place these headings. The way the three major speakers are identified also varies widely. In this guide, you'll find suggested transitions from speaker to speaker based on how they're often identified.

How allegorical is it?

Throughout Jewish and Christian history, the Song has often been seen primarily as an allegory of God's love for His people, or Christ's love for His bride, the church. In modern times, the book more often has been taken at face value, as a passionate and lyrical celebration of love between man and woman. Any allegorical aspect has been dismissed or downplayed.

To some degree this is simply a matter of putting first things first. The poetry was probably originally written for wedding celebrations. Its first meaning is about human love. "There may be more than the literal, but that is not up for discussion until the meaning of the plain sense of the text is accepted."[6]

13

Some of the current resistance to an allegorical interpretation of the Song has been a reaction against seemingly wild excesses of this approach in the past. Today, many aim for an interpretation that focuses on the first meaning of the poems while remaining cautiously open to a secondary allegorical interpretation. Recognizing the historical tradition of viewing the Song allegorically, this guide includes some modern allegorical commentary on the Song.

In our study here, we want to be fully aware of what the Song of Solomon tells us about marital love and intimacy, but also allow ourselves to be pointed toward a higher dimension. Human beauty and intimacy, as good as they are, can't ultimately satisfy. "This is not to denigrate them, but rather to recognize them for what they are. They are pointers to another world, another dimension."[7] As Paul tells us in Ephesians 5, God created sexual love to point beyond itself to a glorious eternal reality. While they shout about human love, the lyrics in the Song of Solomon also whisper to us about God.

1. Tom Gledhill, *The Message of the Song of Songs*, The Bible Speaks Today (Downers Grove, IL: InterVarsity, 1994), 27.
2. Edward J. Young, quoted in J. A. Balchin, "The Song of Solomon," in *The New Bible Commentary*, rev. ed., ed. D. Guthrie and J. A. Motyer (Grand Rapids, MI: Eerdmans, 1970), 579.
3. Gledhill, *Song of Songs*, 20.
4. Leland Ryken and Philip Graham Ryken, eds., *The Literary Study Bible* (Wheaton, IL: Crossway, 2007), introduction to Song of Solomon, "The book at a glance."
5. Tremper Longman III, *Song of Songs*, New International Commentary on the Old Testament (Grand Rapids, MI: Eerdmans, 2001), 14.
6. Dennis F. Kinlaw, "Song of Songs," in *Psalms, Proverbs, Ecclesiastes, Song of Songs*, Expositor's Bible Commentary, vol. 5, ed. Frank E. Gabelein (Grand Rapids, MI: Zondervan, 1990), 1205.
7. Gledhill, *Song of Songs*, 14.

SONG OF SOLOMON: AN OVERVIEW

The Biblical Big Picture

*I am my beloved's
and my beloved is mine.*

SONG 6:3

1. For getting the most from the Song of Solomon, one of the best guidelines is found in 2 Timothy 3:16-17, words which Paul wrote with the Old Testament first in view. He said that all Scripture is of great benefit to (a) teach us, (b) rebuke us, (c) correct us, and (d) train us in righteousness. Paul added that these Scriptures completely equip the person of God "for every good work." As you think seriously about those guidelines, in which of these areas do you especially want to experience the usefulness of the Song of Solomon? Express your desire in a written prayer to God.

   _____

   _____

   _____

   _____

2. In Jeremiah 23:29, God says that His Word is "like fire" and "like a hammer." He can use the Scriptures to burn away unclean thoughts and desires in our hearts. He can also use Scripture, with hammer-like hardness, to crush and crumble our spiritual hardness. From your study of the Song of Solomon, how do you most want to see the fire-and-hammer power of God's Word at work in your own life and marriage? Again, express this longing in a written prayer to God.

_____

_____

_____

_____

3. Think about these words of Paul to his younger helper Timothy: "Do your best to present your-self to God as one approved, a worker who does not need to be ashamed and who correctly handles the word of truth" (2 Timothy 2:15). As you study God's Word of Truth in the Song of Solomon, He calls you to be a "worker." It takes *work*—concentration and perseverance—to fully appropriate God's blessings for us in this book. Express here your commitment before God to work diligently in this study of the Song of Solomon.

_____

_____

_____

_____

4. In one sitting, read through all of the Song of Solomon. Read at a steady pace, and don't worry about anything you don't understand; just keep reading to get a fresh overview of this short book as a whole. From this quick read-ing, what are your strongest impressions of the book?

_____

_____

_____

_____

5. a. Glance again through the pages of the
Song of Solomon, and notice the repeated
phrases—which is typical of many songs.
What repeated phrases, images, or ideas do
you find in these sets of verses?

2:6; 8:3 _____

_____

_____

2:7; 3:5; 5:8; 8:4 _____

_____

_____

2:16; 6:3; 7:10 _____

_____

_____

4:1; 5:12 _____

_____

_____

b. What other notable repetitions do you find?

_____

_____

_____

_____

6. How would you define *love* as this word is used
in the Song of Solomon? Look in particular at
1:2, 2:4, 3:5, 4:10, and 8:6-7.

_____

_____

_____

_____

_____

7. Look carefully at the words of Proverbs 5:15-19. How would you compare that passage's teaching with the theme of the Song of Solomon?

_____

_____

_____

_____

8. Review the Bible's first words regarding sexuality and marriage in the following passages from Genesis. How does the teaching in each of these passages form a foundation for the theme of the Song of Solomon? And what other relationship, if any, do you see between the two?

Genesis 1:27-18 _____

_____

_____

Genesis 2:18,21-23 _____

_____

_____

Genesis 2:24-25 _____

_____

_____

Much of the Song of Solomon reads as if it were taking place in Eden at the time of Genesis 2:18-25. There is an innocent exuberance to the writer's experience of human love that hearkens back to before the Fall.

9. Each of the following Old Testament passages deals in some way with marriage. In what ways does each one relate to the theme and message of the Song of Solomon?

Proverbs 18:22 _____

_____

_____

Proverbs 19:14_____

_____

_____

Malachi 2:13-16_____

_____

_____

Marriage's Biblical Glory

"Old Testament Hebrew has no word for a bachelor. There were not supposed to be any."[1] Abraham, Isaac, Moses, and the other great figures of the Old Testament were all married. Jeremiah was the only prophet we know of who was definitely unmarried. The priests were married. The high priest — the one person who could enter the Holy of Holies, the throne room of God — was married.

The sign of an Israelite man's commitment to God was circumcision, a surgery performed at the point of his intimate contact with his wife. This too was a sign that the act of marriage was holy.

Weddings play a key role in the Bible. The story of man begins with the union of Adam and Eve (see Genesis 2:18-25) and climaxes with the marriage supper of the Lamb (see Revelation 19:6-10). Jesus begins His earthly ministry with a miracle at a wedding (see John 2:1-11). John the Baptist calls Jesus the Bridegroom (see John 3:29-30). Jesus described His time on earth as an engagement

(continued on page 20)

(continued from page 19)
party. Paul says human marriage exists to help us understand the marriage of Christ with the church (see Ephesians 5:25-33).

10. In the New Testament, each of the following passages also deals in some way with marriage. In what ways does each one relate to the theme and message of the Song of Solomon?

1 Corinthians 7:1-5 _____

_____

_____

1 Corinthians 7:10-11 _____

_____

_____

Ephesians 5:21-24 _____

_____

_____

Ephesians 5:25-33 _____

_____

_____

Colossians 3:18 _____

_____

_____

Colossians 3:19 _____

_____

_____

Hebrews 13:4_____

_____

_____

1 Peter 3:1-6 _____

_____

_____

1 Peter 3:7 _____

_____

_____

Matthew 5:31-32 _____

_____

_____

Matthew 19:1-9 _____

_____

_____

The Song of Solomon is wildly enthusiastic about sexual love, and it takes for granted that this sexual intimacy will take place within a faithful marriage. The ancient Israelites who first heard these poems had a strict moral code. Premarital sex was forbidden. If two people had premarital sex anyway, they had to get married, and the man had to pay the bride-price to the woman's parents (see Exodus 22:16). Adultery was a sin so serious that it carried a potential death penalty (see Leviticus 20:10), because it involved breaking a precious covenant relationship.

Far from weakening this moral code, Jesus upped the ante by saying that God judges not just extramarital acts but even extramarital thoughts (see Matthew 5:28).

21

For Thought and Discussion: How important is sexual satisfaction in marriage?

So the Song of Solomon is not about free love. Still, it isn't a "moral social tract"[2] either. It celebrates true love, which is "as strong as death" (Song 8:6).

11. In the following Old Testament passages, the love between God and His people is compared to that between a bridegroom and bride. Look up these passages, and explain the part each could play in your interpretation of the Song of Solomon.

   Isaiah 54:4-8 _____

   _____

   _____

   Jeremiah 2:1-2 _____

   _____

   _____

   Ezekiel 16:8 _____

   _____

   _____

   Hosea 2:14-20 _____

   _____

   _____

12. Also review carefully Paul's New Testament teaching in Ephesians 5:22 and 5:25-32, which compares Christ's relationship to the church with that of a husband and wife. How might this passage play a part in your interpretation of the Song of Solomon?

   _____

   _____

   _____

   _____

Human marriage can be a window into heavenly reality. The apostle Paul tells husbands to love their wives as Christ loves the church (see Ephesians 5:25-27). When he speaks of the union of husband and wife as one flesh, he says, "This is a profound mystery—but I am talking about Christ and the church" (5:32). Such words authorize us to reflect on the Song of Solomon in light of the love between Christ and the church.

For Thought and Discussion: In what ways should human love mirror God's love for His people?

13. From this quick overview of biblical teaching on marriage, what would you say are the most important principles to keep in mind as you seek to better understand the Song of Solomon?

_____

_____

_____

_____

14. It has been stated that because of the uniqueness of the Song of Solomon as a book in the Bible, it requires "a special sensitivity in the reader."[3] How would you describe that requirement? What kind of sensitivity on your part is needed as you explore this book?

_____

_____

_____

_____

"The purity and sacredness of love represented here [in the Song of Solomon] . . . are greatly needed in our day

For Thought and Discussion: In what ways might it be helpful for Christians to seek a biblical perspective on the passion of married love?

where distorted attitudes about love and marriage are commonplace. God created sex and intimacy, and they are holy and good when enjoyed within the bounds of marriage. A husband and wife honor God when they love and enjoy each other."[4]

15. As a further initial exercise in getting familiar with the Song, read through the following verses and record how each of the lovers is viewed. Again, don't worry at this point about trying to understand the imagery more deeply. Just record what you see.

a. How the woman is referred to or perceived:

1:9 _____

_____

1:15 _____

_____

2:2 _____

_____

2:10 _____

_____

2:13 _____

_____

b. How the man is referred to or perceived:

1:16 _____

_____

2:3 _____

_____

2:8 _____

_____

2:9 _____

_____

2:14 _____

_____

2:16 _____

_____

2:17 _____

_____

c. How the woman perceives herself:

1:5 _____

_____

2:1 _____

_____

For the group

In your first meeting, it may be helpful to turn to the front of this book and review together the section titled "How to Use This Guide" on pages 5–9.

You may want to focus your discussion for lesson 1 especially on these concepts, which are emphasized in the lesson's questions:

- God's design for marriage
- The role of sexuality in marriage
- The highest purposes in marriage
- God's love for His people
- Marriage as a reflection of God's love for us

Look also at the questions in the margins under the heading "For Thought and Discussion."

1. Dennis F. Kinlaw, "Song of Songs," in *Psalms, Proverbs, Ecclesiastes, Song of Songs*, Expositor's Bible Commentary, vol. 5, ed. Frank E. Gabelein (Grand Rapids, MI: Zondervan, 1990), 1207.
2. Tom Gledhill, *The Message of the Song of Songs*, The Bible Speaks Today (Downers Grove, IL: InterVarsity, 1994), 29.

3. *New Geneva Study Bible* (Nashville: Nelson, 1995), introduction to Song of Solomon: "Characteristics and Themes."
4. *Life Application Bible* (Wheaton, IL: Tyndale, 1990), introduction to Song of Solomon: "The Blueprint."

SONG OF SOLOMON 1:1–2:7

Longing

> *I am faint with love.*
>
> SONG 2:5

1:1

Following this brief look at the book's title in 1:1, the rest of our study will proceed through the Song section by section. We'll look at just a small grouping of verses (sometimes only one verse) before moving on. Because of the importance of the imagery throughout this love song, our study will focus on observing and understanding the imagery in each brief section.

Solomon's (1:1). The first verse, more literally, is "The Song of Songs, which is Solomon's" (ESV), though the NIV rendering as "Solomon's Song of Songs" captures well the degree of ambiguity in this phrasing. Solomon's name here could indicate his authorship of the entire book, or some other association of the Song with him.

Song of Songs (1:1). This is variously rendered as the "best of all songs" (MSG), "the most beautiful song of Solomon" (GW), "Solomon's Finest

27

Song" (HCSB), and "Solomon's song of songs, more wonderful than any other" (NLT). Notice how a similar Hebrew construction is used in Genesis 9:25 (literally, "servant of servants"); Exodus 29:37 ("holy of holies"); Deuteronomy 10:14 ("heaven of heavens"); and Ecclesiastes 1:2 ("vanity of vanities"). It is certainly the love song of love songs.

1. What does this book's association with Solomon bring to your mind? What characteristics of Solomon would you expect to somehow be reflected in this book?

_____

_____

_____

_____

2. How does this book's identification as a "song" influence how you interpret and respond to it?

_____

_____

_____

_____

1:2-4a

(From here onward in this guide, various suggestions related to the setting and structure and thematic arrangement of the Song will be indicated after the lead-in phrase "*Setting and Structure.*" Likewise, recognizing that in the intermingling of voices in the Song—*his*, *hers*, and *others*—the precise identification of the speaker is sometimes (though not always) uncertain, various suggestions for identifying the voice will be indicated with each section of the Song, as marked by the lead-in word "*Voice.*")

Setting and Structure: Verses 1:2-7 have been titled "The Bride Confesses Her Love" (ESV). Chapter 1 has been titled "The Young Shulammite Bride and Jerusalem's Daughters" (NASB) and "Love Is Better than Wine" (CEV).

Voice: Verses 1:2-4a are seen as *her* words.

3. a. *Observe:* In 1:2-4a, what are the most prominent metaphors and images?

_____

_____

_____

   b. What is each image being figuratively used to represent?

_____

_____

_____

The poet's style can be called sensuous (having to do with the senses), metaphoric (using imagery like doves, wine, apples, and spices to evoke feelings about the human body and human love), hyperbolic (using exaggeration and grand language to make a point), and pastoral (presenting an idealized version of agricultural life, along with many references to nature).

4. a. *Respond and Reflect:* In 1:2-4a, what qualities or values are being highlighted or suggested in each figurative comparison?

_____

_____

_____

b. What do you find most evocative and delightful in the imagery you observed in these
lines?

_____

_____

_____

_____

More delightful (1:2). Delight is one of the book's
themes.

---

5. The following aspects of marital love have been
pointed to as important themes of the Song of
Solomon. Here in 1:2-4a, in what ways, if any,
do you see them reflected?

Giving of self: _____

_____

_____

Desire:_____

_____

_____

Delight in each other: _____

_____

_____

Commitment: _____

_____

_____

Marriage as a reflection of God's love: _____

_____

_____

30

6. What creative title or heading would you suggest for this section?

_____

_____

_____

_____

1:4b-7

Voice: Verse 1:4b is seen as the words of *others*; the rest of this section is seen as *her* words.

7. a. *Observe:* In 1:4b-7, what are the most prominent metaphors and images?

_____

_____

_____

b. What is each image being figuratively used to represent?

_____

_____

_____

Dark am I (1:5). The woman may be boasting of her unusual and beautiful dark skin. Or she may be apologizing for it. Our culture sees tanned skin as a status symbol, because most workers work indoors and tanning is a leisure activity, but in ancient Israel fair skin may have been a status symbol, because labor was largely outdoors and tanned skin suggested that a woman was only an agricultural laborer.

My mother's sons (1:6). See also the reference to the woman's brothers in 8:8-9, where they speak about their sister. Elsewhere in the Old Testament (such as Genesis 34), brothers are

For Further Study:
Notice the indica-
tion of guardianship
by the brothers over
their sister in 1:6 and
in 8:8-9. How does
this compare with the
actions of brothers
toward their sister
in Genesis 34 and
2 Samuel 13? (Note
also Laban's actions
on behalf of his sister
Rebekah in Genesis
24:29-60.)

**For Thought and
Discussion:** How
important is our
physical appearance
as a factor in our
self-image?

guardians of a woman's sexuality and are
involved in marriage negotiations. Here in the
Song they serve in a similar role.

Vineyards . . . my own vineyard (1:6). The vineyard may be a literal place where grapes are
grown. Literally, the bride did agricultural
work. Metaphorically, "my own vineyard" may
also refer to the bride as a whole person or to
the explicitly sexual part of her. The images in
poetry often work on multiple levels like this. In
some way the bride has neglected herself or her
sexuality.

8. a. *Respond and Reflect:* In 1:4b-7, what qualities or values are being highlighted or suggested in each figurative comparison?

_____

_____

_____

b. What do you find most evocative and delightful in the imagery you observed in this
section?

_____

_____

_____

9. Here in 1:4b-7, in what ways, if any, do you see
the following aspects of marital love reflected?

Giving of self: _____

_____

_____

Desire:_____

_____

_____

_____

Delight in each other: _____

_____

_____

Commitment: _____

_____

_____

Marriage as a reflection of God's love:_____

_____

_____

10. What creative title or heading would you suggest for this section?

_____

_____

_____

_____

1:8-11

Setting and Structure: Verses 1:8–2:7 have been titled "Solomon and His Bride Delight in Each Other" (ESV) and "The Banquet" (NKJV).

Voice: Verses 1:8-10 are seen as *his* words, and verse 1:10 as the words of *others*; alternatively, verse 1:8 might also be the words of *others*.

11. a. *Observe:* In 1:8-11, what are the most prominent metaphors and images?

_____

_____

_____

_____

Optional Application: What are the images, ideas, and values in 1:4b-7 that can have the most personal meaning for you in your own marriage?

For Thought and Discussion: How important is physical attraction as a factor to be considered in a man and woman's relationship?

For Further Study: What perspectives on physical attractiveness are taught in Proverbs 31:30 and 1 Peter 3:3-6, and how do these relate to the message of the Song of Solomon?

For Thought and Discussion: To what extent do you think our ideas of physical attractiveness are culturally determined?

Optional Application: What are the images, ideas, and values in 1:8-11 that can have the most personal meaning for you in your own marriage?

b. What is each image being figuratively used to represent?

_____

_____

_____

12. a. *Respond and Reflect:* In 1:8-11, what qualities or values are being highlighted or suggested in each figurative comparison?

_____

_____

_____

b. What do you find most evocative and delightful in the imagery you observed in these lines?

_____

_____

_____

My darling (1:9). In the Song, the man calls the woman "my darling" nine times.

A mare (1:9). "Pairs of stallions were used for the royal vehicles. The presence of a mare among such stallions could be the ultimate distraction. So our lover pays his beloved the ultimate compliment to her sexual attractiveness."[1]

13. Here in 1:8-11, in what ways, if any, do you see the following aspects of marital love reflected?

Giving of self: _____

_____

_____

Desire: _____

34

_____

_____

Delight in each other: _____

_____

_____

Commitment: _____

_____

_____

Marriage as a reflection of God's love: _____

_____

_____

14. What creative title or heading would you suggest for this section?

_____

_____

_____

_____

1:12-17

Voice: Verses 1:12-14 are seen as *her* words. Verse 1:15 is seen as *his* words and verses 1:16-17 as *her* words (alternatively, verse 1:17 might also be *his* words).

15. a. *Observe:* In 1:12-17, what are the most prominent metaphors and images?

_____

_____

_____

_____

b. What is each image being figuratively used to represent?

_____

_____

_____

16. a. *Respond and Reflect:* In 1:12-17, what qualities or values are being highlighted or suggested in each figurative comparison?

_____

_____

_____

b. What do you find most evocative and delightful in the imagery you observed in this section?

_____

_____

_____

17. Here in 1:12-17, in what ways, if any, do you see the following aspects of marital love reflected?

Giving of self: _____

_____

_____

Desire:_____

_____

_____

Delight in each other: _____

_____

_____

Commitment:_____

_____

_____

Marriage as a reflection of God's love: _____

_____

_____

18. What creative title or heading would you suggest for this section?

_____

_____

_____

2:1-2

Voice: Verse 2:1 is seen as *her* words and verse 2:2
as *his* words.

Setting and Structure: Verses 2:1-7 have been titled
"Love Makes Everything Beautiful" (CEV). Chapter 2
has been titled "The Bride's Admiration" (NASB).

19. a. *Observe:* In 2:1-2, what are the most prominent metaphors and images?

_____

_____

_____

b. What is each image being figuratively used to
represent?

_____

_____

_____

20. a. *Respond and Reflect:* In 2:1-2, what qualities
or values are being highlighted or suggested
in each figurative comparison?

_____

_____

_____

b. What do you find most evocative and delightful in the imagery you observed in this section?

_____

_____

_____

In some ways, the setting of the poem resembles Eden with its trees, flowers, birds, and mostly non-predatory animals. The couple makes love not in a house but among the trees. Like Adam and Eve they are naked to each other and unashamed.

21. Here in 2:1-2, in what ways, if any, do you see the following aspects of marital love reflected?

Giving of self: _____

_____

_____

Desire:_____

_____

_____

Delight in each other: _____

_____

_____

Commitment: _____

_____

_____

_____

Marriage as a reflection of God's love: _____

_____

_____

22. What creative title or heading would you suggest for this section?

_____

_____

_____

_____

2:3-7

Voice: Verses 2:3-7 are seen as *her* words.

23. a. *Observe:* In 2:3-7, what are the most prominent metaphors and images?

_____

_____

_____

b. What is each image being figuratively used to
represent?

_____

_____

_____

His fruit is sweet (2:3). "The image . . . has obvious erotic implications, since her lover is identified with that tree."[2] See also 8:5b.

His left arm . . . his right arm (2:6). See the rep-
etition of this image in 8:3. The reader can't be
sure whether the woman has experienced her
lover's touch in this way or if she is imagining
what she desires for the future. The Hebrew has

no time-oriented verbs to tell us if this refers to past memory or future hope.[3]

I charge you (2:7). "In the Hebrew, the daughters are not simply warned but asked to take an oath."[4]

Do not arouse or awaken love until it so desires (2:7). This refrain is found also in 3:5 and 8:4. "Its essence is: 'Do not try to force the situation. Let love take its natural course and its own time.' This refrain creates movement and suspense. The lovers experience separation, hostility, and interference, but the refrain anticipates that the relationship is nevertheless moving forward."[5] The bride enjoys her passions without shame, but she knows that everything should be done in good order, in its appropriate time. Rushing the consummation would spoil the love.

---

24. a. *Respond and Reflect:* In 2:3-7, what qualities or values are being highlighted or suggested in each figurative comparison?

_____

_____

_____

b. What do you find most evocative and delightful in the imagery you observed in these lines?

_____

_____

_____

Like an apple tree (2:3). The poet embraces the whole world when he imagines the body. "The natural landscape, the cycle of the seasons, the beauty of the animal and floral realm, the profusion of goods afforded through trade, the inventive skill of the artisan, the grandeur of cities, are all joyfully affirmed as love is affirmed."[6]

---

25. Here in 2:3-7, in what ways, if any, do you see the following aspects of marital love reflected?

Giving of self: _____

_____

_____

Desire:_____

_____

_____

Delight in each other: _____

_____

_____

Commitment:_____

_____

_____

Marriage as a reflection of God's love: _____

_____

_____

_____

Optional Application: What are the images, ideas, and values in 2:3-7 that can have the most personal meaning for you in your own marriage?

26. What creative title or heading would you suggest for this section?

_____

_____

_____

_____

Summary

27. What would you select as the key verse or passage in this first portion of the Song—the lines that best capture or reflect the dynamics of what this section of the Song is all about?

41

Optional Application: How has your study in chapters 1 and 2 of the Song of Solomon affected your perspective on the passion of married love?

Optional Application: Which passages in chapters 1 and 2 best reflect your own passion for your husband or wife and will be good to keep in mind?

_____

_____

_____

28. List any lingering questions you have about this section (1:1–2:7) in the Song of Solomon.

_____

_____

_____

_____

For the group

Again, you may want to focus your discussion especially on these concepts that are emphasized in the lesson's questions:

- The role of physical attractiveness in marriage
- Joys and tensions in marriage
- The meaning of marriage
- The joy of marital sex
- The permanence of married love

Look also at the questions in the margins under the heading "For Thought and Discussion."

1. Dennis F. Kinlaw, "Song of Songs," in *Psalms, Proverbs, Ecclesiastes, Song of Songs*, Expositor's Bible Commentary, vol. 5, ed. Frank E. Gabelein (Grand Rapids, MI: Zondervan, 1990), 1219.
2. Ariel Bloch and Chana Bloch, *The Song of Songs: A New Translation with an Introduction and Commentary* (Berkeley: University of California Press, 1995), at Song 2:3.
3. Elizabeth Huwiler, "Song of Songs," in *Proverbs, Ecclesiastes, Song of Songs*, by Roland E. Murphy and Elizabeth Huwiler, New International Biblical Commentary (Peabody, MA: Hendrickson, 1999), 227.
4. Huwiler, *Song of Songs*, 228.
5. *New Geneva Study Bible* (Nashville: Nelson, 1995), introduction to Song of Solomon: "Characteristics and Themes."
6. Robert Alter, afterword to *The Song of Songs*, by Bloch and Bloch, 130.

SONG OF SOLOMON 2:8–3:11

Seeking

I looked for the one my heart loves.

SONG 3:1

2:8-13

Setting and Structure: Verses 2:8-17 have been titled "The Bride Adores Her Beloved" (ESV), "The Beloved's Request" (NKJV), and "Winter Is Past" (CEV). Verses 2:8–3:5 have been titled "Memories of Courtship."[1]

In parts of the Song, the couple acts out wedding rituals. Here in chapter 2, the bride is imagining what the groom will do when he arrives for the wedding. His invitation to go with him for a springtime walk (see 2:10-13) is metaphorically an invita-tion to go with him into marriage.

Voice: Verses 2:8-13 are seen as *her* words.

1. a. *Observe:* In 2:8-13, what are the most prominent metaphors and images?

_____

_____

_____

   b. What is each image being figuratively used to
represent?

_____

_____

_____

2. a. *Respond and Reflect:* In 2:8-13, what qualities or values are being highlighted or suggested in each figurative comparison?

_____

_____

_____

   b. What do you find most evocative and delightful in the imagery you observed in this
section?

_____

_____

_____

**There he stands . . . peering through the lat-
tice** (2:9). Is this a stag at the window, or the
bridegroom? It is both, as the poet compares
the one to the other. The bridegroom is part of
the natural world, and the whole of nature is
in tune with the lovers as they step out into a
springtime walk.

---

3. Here in 2:8-13, in what ways, if any, do you see
the following aspects of marital love reflected?

Giving of self: _____

_____

_____

_____

Desire:_____

_____

_____

Delight in each other: _____

_____

_____

_____

Commitment: _____

_____

_____

_____

Marriage as a reflection of God's love: _____

_____

_____

_____

4. What creative title or heading would you suggest for this section?

_____

_____

_____

_____

_____

Optional Application: What are the images, ideas, and values in 2:8-13 that can have the most personal meaning for you in your own marriage?

Stag at the Lattice

The best and highest realities in the love of man and woman can point us even higher, to the highest of all loves. This portion of the Song (2:8-11) can point to our Lord's love for us, and how He seeks our faith.

Our Lover stands at the window of our soul like a "graceful gazelle" or a "mighty stag."[2] He longs for us, but He doesn't batter down our soul's wall or even the lattice that screens the window. Instead, He invites us to peer through the holes in the lattice to glimpse His beauty and strength. We lack the power to throw down the lattice, and if He fully revealed Himself to us, we would be overcome. But we can glimpse Him.

"He comes. He entices. Yet, he ever respects our space. He stands behind the wall, yet uses all the openings to call us forth: a sight, a light, a touch, an odor of sweetness. How hard it is to believe that the Lover eagerly peers in, gazes upon us with love, that we are of such interest to this Divine Being, the delight of his eyes.... Let us have the courage to come out from behind our walls, our defensiveness, to believe in this love, to be open and vulnerable to all the ravishments of Divine Love."[3]

He doesn't force Himself on us, as He could do. He invites us to open to Him.

The Scriptures give voice to the Lover as He calls to us: "Arise, my darling, my beautiful one, come with me" (2:10).

2:14-15

Voice: Verses 2:14-15 are seen as *her* words, or possibly as *his* words.

5. a. *Observe:* In 2:14-15, what are the most prominent metaphors and images?

_____

_____

_____

_____

b. What is each image being figuratively used to represent?

_____

_____

_____

_____

_____

For Further Study: Compare the image of foxes in the vineyard (see Song 2:15) with the scene recorded in Judges 21:2-22.

In the hiding places (2:14). The woman hides teasingly from the man, and he coaxes her out.

Catch (2:15). "Just as the two lovers are about to surrender themselves to each other and forget the world," they have to pay attention to the world. The poet appeals "to outsiders to prevent 'the foxes,' those forces that could destroy the purity of their love, from defiling their vineyards."[4]

Optional Application: What are the images, ideas, and values in 2:14-15 that can have the most personal meaning for you in your own marriage?

6. a. *Respond and Reflect:* In 2:14-15, what qualities or values are being highlighted or suggested in each figurative comparison?

_____

_____

_____

_____

b. What do you find most evocative and delightful in the imagery you observed in this section?

_____

_____

_____

_____

7. Here in 2:14-15, in what ways, if any, do you see the following aspects of marital love reflected?

Giving of self: _____

_____

_____

Desire:_____

_____

_____

Delight in each other: _____

_____

_____

Commitment: _____

_____

_____

Marriage as a reflection of God's love: _____

_____

_____

8. What creative title or heading would you suggest for this section?

_____

_____

_____

_____

2:16-17

Voice: Verses 2:16-17 are seen as *her* words.

9. a. *Observe:* In 2:16-17, what are the most prominent metaphors and images?

_____

_____

_____

_____

b. What is each image being figuratively used to represent?

_____

_____

_____

_____

Optional Application: What are the images, ideas, and values in 2:16-17 that can have the most personal meaning for you in your own marriage?

10. a. *Respond and Reflect:* In 2:16-17, what qualities or values are being highlighted or suggested in each figurative comparison?

_____

_____

_____

_____

b. What do you find most evocative and delightful in the imagery you observed in this section?

_____

_____

_____

_____

_____

My beloved is mine and I am his (2:16). A refrain like this recurs in 6:3 and 7:10. The three versions have subtle differences. This first time, the woman speaks of mutual commitment.

49

11. Here in 2:16-17, in what ways, if any, do you see the following aspects of marital love reflected?

Giving of self: _____

_____

_____

Desire:_____

_____

_____

Delight in each other: _____

_____

_____

Commitment: _____

_____

_____

Marriage as a reflection of God's love: _____

_____

_____

12. What creative title or heading would you suggest for this section?

_____

_____

_____

_____

3:1-5

Setting and Structure: Verses 3:1-5 have been titled "The Bride's Dream" (ESV), "A Troubled Night" (NKJV), and "Beautiful Dreams" (CEV). Chapter 3 has been titled "The Bride's Troubled Dream" (NASB).

Voice: Verses 3:1-5 are seen as *her* words.

13. How would you summarize what happens in 3:1-4, as narrated here?

_____

_____

_____

_____

14. a. *Observe:* In 3:1-5, what are the most prominent metaphors and images?

_____

_____

_____

_____

b. What is each image being figuratively used to represent?

_____

_____

_____

_____

For Further Study: Keeping in mind the image of the woman bringing the husband to her mother's house, look at Genesis 2:24 and 24:67. What possible connection do you see?

Optional Application: Keeping in mind the Song's refrain, "Do not arouse or awaken love until it so desires" (3:5), what are the practical steps a man or woman can take to adhere to this wisdom?

Optional Application: What are the images, ideas, and values in 3:1-5 that can have the most personal meaning for you in your own marriage?

All night long (3:1). Her lover fills the woman's thoughts all day and even her nightly dreams. "The girl dreams about her wedding and the lovemaking that will follow. There is everything that we might expect here: erotic reveries, nightmares, fears of losing her lover, and romantic experiences that transform him into a prince. In her dreams, the girl's wedding becomes a splendid, royal occasion, and the lover is identified with Solomon himself."[5]

Watchmen (3:3). These watchmen appear again, with violent involvement, in 5:7.

Till I had brought him to my mother's house (3:4). To bring him to her mother's house means to marry him. She isn't imagining

51

sneaking him in for an illicit tryst. "Consummation she wants, but even in her dream she wants that consummation to be right. Where in human literature does one find a text so erotic and yet so moral as this?"[6]

15. a. *Respond and Reflect:* In 3:1-5, what qualities or values are being highlighted or suggested in each figurative comparison?

    _____

    _____

    _____

    _____

   b. What do you find most evocative and delightful in the imagery you observed in these lines?

    _____

    _____

    _____

    _____

16. Here in 3:1-5, in what ways, if any, do you see the following aspects of marital love reflected?

   Giving of self: _____

    _____

    _____

   Desire:_____

    _____

    _____

   Delight in each other: _____

    _____

    _____

   Commitment: _____

52

_____

_____

Marriage as a reflection of God's love: _____

_____

_____

17. What creative title or heading would you suggest for this section?

_____

_____

_____

_____

3:6-8

Setting and Structure: Verses 3:6-11 have been titled "Solomon Arrives for the Wedding" (ESV) and "The Groom and the Wedding Party" (CEV). Verses 3:6–5:1 have been titled "The Coming of Solomon" (NKJV).

Voice: Verses 3:6-8 are seen as *her* words.

18. a. *Observe:* In 3:6-8, what are the most prominent metaphors and images?

_____

_____

_____

_____

   b. What is each image being figuratively used to represent?

_____

_____

_____

_____

Who is this . . . ? (3:6). Who *is* it? Because of the mention of "Solomon's carriage" in 3:7, it is sometimes assumed at first glance that the approaching person is Solomon. But for grammatical reasons, many interpreters see the woman as the one drawing near. That would mean that the question is rhetorical and verse 7 isn't the answer. Instead, verse 6 announces the woman's dramatic arrival. Similar rhetorical questions are asked in 6:10 and 8:5, and in both cases, "Who is this?" refers to the woman.

Coming up (3:6). Or "rising" like the sun at daybreak.

Solomon's carriage (3:7). Some see this as figurative. To celebrate their own village wedding, the lovers may be singing a piece of a song originally sung at one of Solomon's royal weddings. The couple are like the king and queen of their own marriage feast.[7] Other interpreters envision the woman perfumed and arriving for her wedding in a carriage supplied by the king. Either way, the lovers are finally meeting for the wedding ceremony.

Carriage (3:7). Also variously translated as "litter," "sedan," "couch," and even "bed." It may not be a moving vehicle.

19. a. *Respond and Reflect:* In 3:6-8, what qualities or values are being highlighted or suggested in each figurative comparison?

_____

_____

_____

b. What do you find most evocative and delightful in the imagery you observed in this section?

_____

_____

_____

20. Here in 3:6-8, in what ways, if any, do you see the following aspects of marital love reflected?

Giving of self: _____
_____
_____

Desire:_____
_____
_____

Delight in each other: _____
_____
_____

Commitment: _____
_____
_____

Marriage as a reflection of God's love: _____
_____
_____

21. What creative title or heading would you suggest for this section?

_____
_____
_____
_____

Optional Application: What are the images, ideas, and values in 3:6-8 that can have the most personal meaning for you in your own marriage?

3:9-11

Voice: Verses 3:9-11 are seen as *her* words.

22. a. *Observe:* In 3:9-11, what are the most prominent metaphors and images?

55

Optional Application: What are the images, ideas, and values in 3:9-11 that can have the most personal meaning for you in your own marriage?

Optional Application: How has your study in chapters 2 and 3 of the Song of Solomon affected your perspective on the passion of married love?

Optional Application: Which passages in chapters 2 and 3 best reflect your own passion for your husband or wife and will be good to keep in mind?

_____

_____

_____

_____

b. What is each image being figuratively used to represent?

_____

_____

_____

_____

Carriage (3:9). This is a different Hebrew word from the one translated as "carriage" in 3:7, and may refer to a different item. The term in 3:9 might be better translated as "pavilion," a *stationary* structure.[8]

---

23. a. *Respond and Reflect:* In 3:9-11, what qualities or values are being highlighted or suggested in each figurative comparison?

_____

_____

_____

_____

b. What do you find most evocative and delightful in the imagery you observed in these lines?

_____

_____

_____

_____

24. Here in 3:9-11, in what ways, if any, do you see the following aspects of marital love reflected?

Giving of self: _____

_____

_____

Desire:_____

_____

_____

Delight in each other: _____

_____

_____

Commitment: _____

_____

_____

Marriage as a reflection of God's love: _____

_____

_____

25. What creative title or heading would you suggest for this section?

_____

_____

Summary

26. What would you select as the key verse or passage in this portion of the Song—the lines that best capture or reflect the dynamics of what this section of the Song is all about?

_____

_____

_____

_____

_____

27. List any lingering questions you have about chapters 2 and 3 in the Song of Solomon.

_____

_____

_____

_____

For the group

Again, you may want to focus your discussion especially on these concepts that are emphasized in the lesson's questions:

- The role of physical attractiveness in marriage
- Joys and tensions in marriage
- The meaning of marriage
- The joy of marital sex
- The permanence of married love

1. *Life Application Bible* (Wheaton, IL: Tyndale, 1990).
2. M. Basil Pennington, *The Song of Songs: A Spiritual Commentary* (Woodstock, VT: SkyLight Paths, 2004), 45.
3. Pennington, *Song of Songs*, 47.
4. Dennis F. Kinlaw, "Song of Songs," in *Psalms, Proverbs, Ecclesiastes, Song of Songs*, Expositor's Bible Commentary, vol. 5, ed. Frank E. Gabelein (Grand Rapids, MI: Zondervan, 1990), 1224.
5. *New Geneva Study Bible* (Nashville: Nelson, 1995), introduction to Song of Solomon: "Characteristics and Themes."
6. Kinlaw, *Song of Songs*, 1225.
7. Tom Gledhill, *The Message of the Song of Songs*, The Bible Speaks Today (Downers Grove, IL: InterVarsity, 1994), 150–151.
8. Ariel Bloch and Chana Bloch, *The Song of Songs: A New Translation with an Introduction and Commentary* (Berkeley: University of California Press, 1995), at Song 3:7 and 3:9.

SONG OF SOLOMON 4

Finding

*Let my beloved come into his garden
and taste its choice fruits.*

SONG 4:16

1. Proverbs 2:1-5 tells about the sincere person who truly longs for wisdom and understanding, and who searches the Scriptures for it—as if there were treasure hidden there. Such a person, this passage says, will come to understand the fear of the Lord and discover the knowledge of God. As you continue exploring the Song of Solomon, what "hidden treasure" would you like God to help you find here—to show you what God and His wisdom are really like? If you have this desire, how would you express it in your own words of prayer to God?

_____

_____

_____

_____

_____

_____

For Thought and Discussion: How concerned should we be about our own physical attractiveness?

4:1-3

In 3:6-10 of the Song, the wedding takes place at last. Now the jubilant bridegroom extols his bride's beauty in 4:1-7. He anticipates their physical union in 4:12-15. The bride invites him in 4:16, and they consummate the marriage in 5:1.

As was the custom in ancient Israel, the bride is veiled (see 4:1). But her husband is now free to see and enjoy her body, and he details what he sees part by part. The imagery (sheep, pomegranate, tower of David) may seem foreign today, but the overall effect remains powerful.

Setting and Structure: Verses 4:1–5:1 have been titled "Solomon Admires His Bride's Beauty" (ESV) and "What a Beautiful Bride" (CEV). Chapter 4 has been titled "Solomon's Love Expressed" (NASB).

Voice: Verses 4:1-3 are seen as *his* words.

2. a. *Observe:* In 4:1-3, what are the most prominent metaphors and images?

_____

_____

_____

b. What is each image being figuratively used to represent?

_____

_____

_____

_____

Like the halves of a pomegranate (4:3). "The literal meaning of the Hebrew is 'a pomegranate slice,' so the image evidently suggests the section of a delicately curving contour. . . . But if the pomegranate is adopted as an image for the cheek chiefly because of the pleasing curve, it has also been chosen because of the gustatory association with luscious, tangy fruit."[1]

3. a. *Respond and Reflect:* In 4:1-3, what qualities or values are being highlighted or suggested in each figurative comparison?

   _____

   _____

   _____

   _____

   b. What do you find most evocative and delightful in the imagery you observed in this section?

   _____

   _____

   _____

   _____

4. Here in 4:1-3, in what ways, if any, do you see the following aspects of marital love reflected?

   Giving of self: _____

   _____

   _____

   Desire:_____

   _____

   _____

   Delight in each other: _____

   _____

Optional Application: How important is it to express our appreciation of our spouse's physical appearance? Why is this important in your own relationship? How would you assess yourself in this area?

Optional Application: What are the images, ideas, and values in 4:1-3 that can have the most personal meaning for you in your own marriage?

Commitment: _____

_____

_____

Marriage as a reflection of God's love: _____

_____

_____

5. What creative title or heading would you suggest for this section?

_____

_____

_____

_____

The man's praise of the woman's beauty in 4:1-7 is the first of four such passages; he will praise her again in 6:4-9 and 7:1-9, while the woman praises the man in this way in 5:10-16. Here in 4:1-7, the man inventories her physical charms from her eyes down to her breasts. He is less interested in comparing her body parts to things they look like than he is in evoking the emotions they arouse. Her eyes don't look like doves; they make him feel the way doves make him feel. His imagery is also meant to suggest excellence: the tower of David is the ultimate, perfect tower, for example.

4:4-6

Voice: Verses 4:4-6 are seen as *his* words.

6. a. *Observe:* In 4:4-6, what are the most prominent metaphors and images?

_____

_____

_____

_____

b. What is each image being figuratively used to
represent?

_____

_____

_____

_____

7. a. *Respond and Reflect:* In 4:4-6, what qualities
or values are being highlighted or suggested
in each figurative comparison?

_____

_____

_____

_____

b. What do you find most evocative and delightful in the imagery you observed in these
lines?

_____

_____

_____

_____

8. Here in 4:4-6, in what ways, if any, do you see
the following aspects of marital love reflected?

**Optional
Application:** What
are the images, ideas,
and values in 4:4-6
that can have the
most personal mean-
ing for you in your
own marriage?

Giving of self: _____

_____

_____

Desire:_____

_____

_____

Delight in each other: _____

_____

_____

Commitment: _____

_____

_____

Marriage as a reflection of God's love: _____

_____

_____

9. How do you see the man's description of the woman's body in 4:1-6 as a reflection of the creation doctrine that all that God made was "very good" (Genesis 1:31)?

_____

_____

_____

_____

10. What creative title or heading would you suggest for this section?

_____

_____

_____

_____

Beautiful Bride

Once again we let the glorious love of man and woman point our gaze to an even higher love. In the lover's praise of his beloved, we hear the Lord's delight in the beauty of His bride, the church. Her beauty is pure, like doves. It is strong, like the tower of David. It is fruitful, like the pomegranate. The Lover invites His bride to leave off longing for any lesser suitors and to seek her fulfillment in His delight alone. She need no longer wonder anxiously if she is beautiful enough, strong enough, pure enough. He declares that she is enough. She need no longer preen or show off to prove that she has beauty and worth. His praise sweeps aside her vanity and self-importance. She can finally rest and respond to His loving gaze.

4:7-8

Voice: Verses 4:7-8 are seen as *his* words.

11. a. *Observe:* In 4:7-8, what are the most prominent metaphors and images?

_____

_____

_____

_____

_____

   b. What is each image being figuratively used to represent?

_____

_____

_____

_____

_____

Lebanon . . . Amana . . . Senir . . . . Hermon
(4:8). These four mountains of the north sym-
bolize "inaccessibility and danger, and . . .
majestic, primeval beauty."[2]

My bride, come with me (4:8). The bridegroom
sees his bride high above him, inaccessible in
figurative mountains. He musters the courage
to invite her to come down from her goddess-
like throne to his ordinary level. He may be
afraid to pursue intimacy with such a majestic
woman. But he overcomes his fears of this dan-
gerous beauty who has captivated him, and he
moves toward her with confidence.

12. a. *Respond and Reflect:* In 4:7-8, what qualities
or values are being highlighted or suggested
in each figurative comparison?

_____

_____

_____

_____

b. What do you find most evocative and delightful in the imagery you observed in this
section?

_____

_____

_____

_____

13. Here in 4:7-8, in what ways, if any, do you see
the following aspects of marital love reflected?

Giving of self: _____

_____

_____

Desire:_____

_____

Delight in each other: _____

_____

_____

Commitment: _____

_____

_____

Marriage as a reflection of God's love: _____

_____

_____

14. What creative title or heading would you suggest for this section?

_____

_____

_____

Optional Application: What are the images, ideas, and values in 4:7-8 that can have the most personal meaning for you in your own marriage?

Come Away with Me

"You are altogether beautiful," the bridegroom says. "Come with me . . . my bride,
come with me . . . descend . . ." (4:8). The man's
invitation can be felt as the Lord's invitation
to us: Come down from the high, aloof perch
where you sit enthroned as a godlike self.
Come down to the lowly place where I, your
Lover, live. Abandon your defenses and pre-
tenses. You have stolen My heart, and I have
given My very life to win you. You are a garden locked up; open to Me.

We may fear to respond, to descend from
the mountain and unlock the garden. We may
feel uncomfortable in the humble place He
asks us to call home. But only our Lover knows
and treasures the richness of the garden we
truly are. We don't really need that lofty temple
we've built to our self-reliance. We need Him.

4:9-11

Voice: Verses 4:9-11 are seen as *his* words.

15. a. *Observe:* In 4:9-11, what are the most prominent metaphors and images?

_____

_____

_____

_____

_____

   b. What is each image being figuratively used to represent?

_____

_____

_____

_____

_____

How delightful is your love (4:10). The Hebrew word for "love" here refers not to the emotion of love, but to the physical act of love. The statement is a "decorous"[3] exclamation of excitement, associated with sensual pleasures like wine, spice, honey, and the opening of a locked garden.

---

16. a. *Respond and Reflect:* In 4:9-11, what qualities or values are being highlighted or suggested in each figurative comparison?

_____

_____

_____

_____

b. What do you find most evocative and delightful in the imagery you observed in these lines?

_____

_____

_____

_____

Optional Application: What are the images, ideas, and values in 4:9-11 that can have the most personal meaning for you in your own marriage?

17. Here in 4:9-11, in what ways, if any, do you see the following aspects of marital love reflected?

Giving of self: _____

_____

_____

Desire: _____

_____

_____

Delight in each other: _____

_____

_____

Commitment: _____

_____

_____

Marriage as a reflection of God's love: _____

_____

_____

18. What creative title or heading would you suggest for this section?

_____

_____

_____

_____

4:12-15

Voice: Verses 4:12-15 are seen as *his* words.

19. a. *Observe:* In 4:12-15, what are the most prominent metaphors and images?

_____

_____

_____

_____

_____

 b. What is each image being figuratively used to represent?

_____

_____

_____

_____

_____

20. a. *Respond and Reflect:* In 4:12-15, what qualities or values are being highlighted or suggested in each figurative comparison?

_____

_____

_____

_____

_____

 b. What do you find most evocative and delightful in the imagery you observed in this section?

_____

_____

_____

_____

_____

All the finest spices (4:14). The woman's body excites her husband's senses like fragrant spices, perfume, and succulent fruit. By listing specific spices and plants familiar to ancient Israel, the poet also evokes the impression that the lovers are consummating their love in a garden full of those fragrances. They are in a garden, and the woman's body is a garden.

Instead of writing about sex explicitly, the poet uses "the reticence of symbolism"[4] to evoke it. He conveys the idea that the couple is laying claim to something of exquisite value— not something dull or mundane to be practiced thoughtlessly or something to be ashamed of.

---

21. Here in 4:12-15, in what ways, if any, do you see the following aspects of marital love reflected?

Giving of self: _____

_____

_____

Desire: _____

_____

_____

Delight in each other: _____

_____

_____

Commitment: _____

_____

_____

Marriage as a reflection of God's love: _____

_____

Optional Application: What are the images, ideas, and values in 4:12-15 that can have the most personal meaning for you in your own marriage?

For Further Study: Observe how all the five senses are employed in the Song: *taste* (see 2:3; 4:16; 5:1; 7:9); *smell* (see 1:3; 1:12; 3:6; 4:10-11); *touch* (see 1:2; 2:6; 3:4; 8:3); *hearing* (see 2:14; 5:2; 8:13); and *sight* (see 1:6; 2:14; 4:9; 6:5; 6:13).

_____

_____

22. What creative title or heading would you suggest for this section?

_____

_____

_____

_____

_____

4:16

Voice: Verse 4:16 is seen as *her* words, though the opening lines about the wind might be a continuation of *his* words in 4:1-15.

23. a. *Observe:* In 4:16, what are the most prominent metaphors and images?

_____

_____

_____

_____

_____

b. What is each image being figuratively used to represent?

_____

_____

_____

_____

_____

72

24. a. *Respond and Reflect:* In 4:16, what qualities or values are being highlighted or suggested in each figurative comparison?

_____

_____

_____

_____

_____

b. What do you find most evocative and delightful in the imagery you observed in this verse?

_____

_____

_____

_____

_____

Optional Application: In what ways do we need to be aware of how selfishness can play a harmful role in our sexual relationship in marriage?

Optional Application: What are the images, ideas, and values in 4:16 that can have the most personal meaning for you in your own marriage?

Garden (4:16). After consummation, "my garden" is now "his garden." Likewise, "my own vineyard" (1:6) is the lover's vineyard (see 8:12).

---

25. Here in 4:16, in what ways, if any, do you see the following aspects of marital love reflected?

Giving of self: _____

_____

_____

Desire:_____

_____

_____

Delight in each other: _____

_____

Optional Application: How has your study in chapter 4 of the Song of Solomon affected your perspective on the passion of married love?

Optional Application: Which passages in chapter 4 best reflect your own passion for your husband or wife and will be good to keep in mind?

Commitment: _____

_____

_____

Marriage as a reflection of God's love: _____

_____

_____

_____

26. What creative title or heading would you suggest for this verse?

_____

_____

_____

_____

Summary

27. What would you select as the key verse or passage in this portion of the Song—the lines that best capture or reflect the dynamics of what this section of the Song is all about?

_____

_____

_____

_____

28. List any lingering questions you have about chapter 4 in the Song of Solomon.

_____

_____

_____

For the group

Again, you may want to focus your discussion especially on these concepts that are emphasized in the lesson's questions:

- The role of physical attractiveness in marriage
- Joys and tensions in marriage
- The meaning of marriage
- The joy of marital sex
- The permanence of married love

Remember to look also at the "Thought and Discussion" question in the margin.

1. Robert Alter, afterword to *The Song of Songs: A New Translation with an Introduction and Commentary*, by Ariel Bloch and Chana Bloch (Berkeley: University of California Press, 1995), 124–125.
2. Ariel Bloch and Chana Bloch, *The Song of Songs: A New Translation with an Introduction and Commentary* (Berkeley: University of California Press, 1995), at 4:8.
3. Alter, afterword to *The Song of Songs*, by Bloch and Bloch, 124.
4. Leland Ryken and Philip Graham Ryken, eds., *The Literary Study Bible* (Wheaton, IL: Crossway, 2007), at Song of Solomon 4:9.

SONG OF SOLOMON 5

Further Finding

> *This is my beloved,*
> *this is my friend.*
>
> SONG 5:16

5:1-3

Setting and Structure: Chapter 5 has been titled "The Torment of Separation" (NASB). Verses 5:2-9 have been titled "The Bride Searches for Her Beloved" (ESV) and "Another Dream" (CEV). Verses 5:2–6:3 have been titled "The Shulamite's Troubled Evening" (NKJV).

Voice: Verse 5:1 is seen as *his* words, except for the last line with its invitation to eat and drink, which is seen as the words of *others*. Verses 5:2-3 are seen as *her* words.

   1. a. *Observe:* In 5:1-3, what are the most prominent metaphors and images?

      _____

      _____

      _____

      _____

b. What is each image being figuratively used to represent?

_____

_____

_____

_____

Eat, friends, and drink; drink your fill of love
(5:1). The couple's friends are now speaking, because their relationship is more than their private business. It has implications for their community. It will affect their family members and others. Their children will affect society. Their relationship to the whole of humanity is different now. This is why even in our culture, a wedding has to be performed in the presence of witnesses. It is also why a wedding is treated as a legal matter, and why the church has a stake in the way marriage is defined and conducted.[1]

2. a. *Respond and Reflect:* In 5:1-3, what qualities or values are being highlighted or suggested in each figurative comparison?

_____

_____

_____

_____

b. What do you find most evocative and delightful in the imagery you observed in these verses?

_____

_____

_____

_____

3. Here in 5:1-3, in what ways, if any, do you see the following aspects of marital love reflected?

Giving of self: _____
_____
_____

Desire:_____
_____
_____

Delight in each other: _____
_____
_____

Commitment: _____
_____
_____

Marriage as a reflection of God's love: _____
_____
_____

4. What creative title or heading would you suggest for this section?

_____
_____
_____
_____

Optional Application: What are the images, ideas, and values in 5:1-3 that can have the most personal meaning for you in your own marriage?

He was gone (5:6). In 5:2-8, the woman has a bad dream in which she loses the ecstasy she has enjoyed. The dream is about "untaken opportunity"[2] and can be applied to other areas of our lives when we fail to take an opportunity the Lord has offered us.

5. How would you compare the night experience of 5:2-7 with what happened at night in 3:1-4?

_____

_____

_____

_____

5:4-8

Voice: Verses 5:4-8 are seen as *her* words.

6. a. *Observe:* In 5:4-8, what are the most prominent metaphors and images?

_____

_____

_____

_____

b. What is each image being figuratively used to represent?

_____

_____

_____

_____

7. a. *Respond and Reflect:* In 5:4-8, what qualities or values are being highlighted or suggested in each figurative comparison?

_____

_____

_____

_____

_____

b. What do you find most evocative and delightful in the imagery you observed in this section?

_____

_____

_____

_____

The Song began with poems about a couple in love (see 1:9–2:7). The context was courtship, and the wedding followed (see 3:6–5:1). Now after the wedding we have more poems about a couple in love. Some interpreters say the context here is marriage. In 5:2-8, the bride has a frustrating dream about separation from her husband, looking for him all over a city and not finding him.

Other interpreters think the poems in the rest of the Song don't necessarily take place *after* the couple's wedding. The wedding poems in 3:6–5:1 are the center and climax of the Song, but the poems after the climax may not necessarily be about a married couple.

8. Here in 5:4-8, in what ways, if any, do you see the following aspects of marital love reflected?

Giving of self: _____

_____

_____

Desire:_____

_____

_____

**Optional
Application:** What
are the images, ideas,
and values in 5:4-8
that can have the
most personal mean-
ing for you in your
own marriage?

Delight in each other: _____

_____

_____

Commitment: _____

_____

_____

Marriage as a reflection of God's love: _____

_____

_____

9. What creative title or heading would you suggest for this section?

_____

_____

_____

_____

Beat me . . . bruised me (5:7). This beating may
be real or a dream. Either way, for some interpreters it conveys the tension the bride feels
between her passion and the rules of the society around her. Others think it reflects her guilt
over how slowly she responded to her husband.

Love doesn't guarantee constant bliss in
a relationship. When two people are intimate,
they affect each other for good and for ill. There
are times of bliss and times of hurt. One person
is lazy in responding to the other, and there is
a consequence. Men and women are different,
and there is tension. There are misunderstand-
ings and the need to adjust to each other.

5:9

Voice: Verse 5:9 is seen as the words of *others*.

82

10. a. *Observe:* In 5:9, what are the most prominent metaphors and images?

_____

_____

_____

_____

   b. What is each image being figuratively used to represent?

_____

_____

_____

_____

11. a. *Respond and Reflect:* In 5:9, what qualities or values are being highlighted or suggested in each figurative comparison?

_____

_____

_____

_____

_____

   b. What do you find most evocative and delight-ful in the imagery you observed in this verse?

_____

_____

_____

_____

_____

12. Here in 5:9, in what ways, if any, do you see the following aspects of marital love reflected?

   Giving of self: _____

Optional Application: What are the images, ideas, and values in 5:9 that can have the most personal meaning for you in your own marriage?

Desire:_____

Delight in each other: _____

Commitment: _____

Marriage as a reflection of God's love: _____

How is your beloved better? (5:9). This question
invites the song of praise in 5:10-16. Compare
the question at the end of chapter 6, which
introduces the praise in chapter 7.

13. What creative title or heading would you suggest for this verse?

_____

_____

_____

5:10-11

Song 5:10-16 is the only passage where
the bride describes her lover. Just as he

inventoried her eyes, lips, neck, and so on, she also inventories his body from head down to legs and then back to mouth. This kind of inventory of the male body from a woman's point of view is rare in ancient literature. She uses images of "sculptural or architectural solidity" denoting strength, as well as images of "tenderness and sweetness."[3] Her description has elements of fantasy understandable from a woman overwhelmed with love. He is her ultimate man.

Setting and Structure: Verses 5:10–6:1 have been titled "The Bride Praises Her Beloved" (ESV).

Voice: Verses 5:10-11 are seen as *her* words.

14. a. *Observe:* In 5:10-11, what are the most prominent metaphors and images?

_____

_____

_____

_____

_____

    b. What is each image being figuratively used to represent?

_____

_____

_____

_____

_____

15. a. *Respond and Reflect:* In 5:10-11, what qualities or values are being highlighted or suggested in each figurative comparison?

Optional Application: What are the images, ideas, and values in 5:10-11 that can have the most personal meaning for you in your own marriage?

For Further Study: Compare the description in 5:10-16 with the description of Jerusalem's princes in Lamentations 4:7, and with the descriptions of David in 1 Samuel 16:12 and 17:42. What do they say about the ideal of manly attractiveness in ancient Israel?

_____

_____

_____

_____

_____

b. What do you find most evocative and delightful in the imagery you observed in this section?

_____

_____

_____

_____

_____

16. Here in 5:10-11, in what ways, if any, do you see the following aspects of marital love reflected?

Giving of self: _____

_____

_____

Desire: _____

_____

_____

Delight in each other: _____

_____

_____

Commitment: _____

_____

_____

Marriage as a reflection of God's love: _____

_____

_____

17. What creative title or heading would you suggest for this section?

_____

_____

_____

_____

5:12-13

Voice: Verses 5:12-13 are seen as *her* words.

18. a. *Observe:* In 5:12-13, what are the most prominent metaphors and images?

_____

_____

_____

_____

b. What is each image being figuratively used to represent?

_____

_____

_____

_____

19. a. *Respond and Reflect:* In 5:12-13, what qualities or values are being highlighted or suggested in each figurative comparison?

_____

_____

_____

_____

_____

b. What do you find most evocative and delightful in the imagery you observed in these lines?

_____

_____

_____

_____

_____

20. Here in 5:12-13, in what ways, if any, do you see the following aspects of marital love reflected?

Giving of self: _____

_____

_____

Desire:_____

_____

_____

Delight in each other: _____

_____

_____

_____

Commitment: _____

_____

_____

_____

Marriage as a reflection of God's love: _____

_____

_____

_____

21. What creative title or heading would you suggest for this section?

_____

_____

_____

_____

Optional Application: What are the images, ideas, and values in 5:12-13 that can have the most personal meaning for you in your own marriage?

My Beloved, My Friend

Again we look beyond the words of a woman speaking of her human lover and consider how our own heart (or the church as a whole) speaks of our divine Lover. "How is your beloved better than others?" (5:9) the world asks us. How do we respond?

He is beyond the ten thousand other gods that vie for our attention. Idols may be made of gold, ivory, marble, and gems, but our Lover has the beauty and strength of these in a body that was broken for our sake and raised from death imperishable. Others have feet of clay, but He has legs of marble on feet of pure gold — solid, pure, majestic. His eyes are like doves when they turn toward us in mercy and delight. His mouth is sweetness itself when it invites us to follow where He leads. When we turn toward Him and look at Him — truly look and see Him — we are awed, overwhelmed, humbled. This is our Beloved. This is our Friend, the true friend of our souls, the one who knows us, hears us, sees us. The one we can trust.

5:14-16

Voice: Verses 5:14-16 are seen as *her* words.

22. a. *Observe:* In 5:14-16, what are the most prominent metaphors and images?

_____

_____

_____

_____

b. What is each image being figuratively used to represent?

_____

_____

_____

_____

23. a. *Respond and Reflect:* In 5:14-16, what qualities or values are being highlighted or suggested in each figurative comparison?

_____

_____

_____

_____

b. What do you find most evocative and delightful in the imagery you observed in this section?

_____

_____

_____

_____

___

Like Lebanon (5:15). A "symbol of majesty" that evokes the mountain as well as "towering cedar trees, lush vegetation, wine, and sweet fragrance."[4]

___

24. Here in 5:14-16, in what ways, if any, do you see the following aspects of marital love reflected?

Giving of self: _____

_____

_____

Desire:_____

_____

_____

Delight in each other: _____

_____

_____

Commitment: _____

_____

_____

Marriage as a reflection of God's love: _____

_____

_____

Optional Application: What are the images, ideas, and values in 5:14-16 that can have the most personal meaning for you in your own marriage?

25. How do you see the woman's description of the man's body in 5:10-16 as a reflection of the creation doctrine that everything God made was "very good" (Genesis 1:31)?

_____

_____

_____

_____

_____

This is my beloved (5:16). The triumphant conclusion to her catalog of her lover's excellencies. She dares anyone to disagree.

This is my friend (5:16). He is her lover, and she doesn't shy away from talking about him in erotic terms. But she's not content with a physical relationship alone. He is also her friend; he knows her, she trusts him. She enjoys the inside of him as well as the outside.

Optional Application: How has your study in chapter 5 of the Song of Solomon affected your perspective on the passion of married love?

Optional Application: Which passages in chapter 5 best reflect your own passion for your husband or wife and will be good to keep in mind?

26. What creative title or heading would you suggest for this section?

_____

_____

_____

_____

Summary

27. What would you select as the key verse or passage in chapter 5 of the Song—the lines that best capture or reflect the dynamics of what this section of the Song is all about?

_____

_____

_____

_____

28. List any lingering questions you have about chapter 5 in the Song of Solomon.

_____

_____

_____

_____

For the group

Again, you may want to focus your discussion especially on these concepts that are emphasized in the lesson's questions:

- The role of physical attractiveness in marriage
- Joys and tensions in marriage
- The meaning of marriage
- The joy of marital sex
- The permanence of married love

1. Dennis F. Kinlaw, "Song of Songs," in *Psalms, Proverbs, Ecclesiastes, Song of Songs*, Expositor's Bible Commentary, vol. 5, ed. Frank E. Gabelein (Grand Rapids, MI: Zondervan, 1990), 1220–1221.
2. J. A. Balchin, "The Song of Solomon," in *The New Bible Commentary*, rev. ed., ed. D. Guthrie and J. A. Motyer (Grand Rapids, MI: Eerdmans, 1970), 579.
3. Ariel Bloch and Chana Bloch, *The Song of Songs: A New Translation with an Introduction and Commentary* (Berkeley: University of California Press, 1995), at Song 5:10.
4. Bloch and Bloch, *The Song of Songs*, at Song 5:15.

SONG OF SOLOMON 6

Enjoying

Your eyes . . . overwhelm me.

SONG 6:5

6:1-3

Setting and Structure: Verses 6:2-3 have been titled "Together in the Garden of Love" (ESV). Chapter 6 has been titled "Mutual Delight in Each Other" (NASB).

Voice: Verse 6:1 is seen as the words of *others*; verses 6:2-3 are seen as *her* words.

1. a. *Observe:* In 6:1-3, what are the most prominent metaphors and images?

   _____

   _____

   _____

   _____

   b. What is each image being figuratively used to represent?

   _____

   _____

_____

_____

2. a. *Respond and Reflect:* In 6:1-3, what qualities
      or values are being highlighted or suggested
      in each figurative comparison?

   _____

   _____

   _____

   _____

   b. What do you find most evocative and delight-
      ful in the imagery you observed in these
      lines?

   _____

   _____

   _____

   _____

3. Here in 6:1-3, in what ways, if any, do you see
   the following aspects of marital love reflected?

   Giving of self: _____

   _____

   _____

   Desire:_____

   _____

   _____

   Delight in each other: _____

   _____

   _____

   Commitment:_____

   _____

   _____

Marriage as a reflection of God's love: _____

_____

_____

_____

4. What creative title or heading would you suggest for this section?

_____

_____

_____

_____

6:4-6

Setting and Structure: Verses 6:4–7:10 have been titled "Solomon and His Bride Delight in Each Other" (ESV). Verses 6:4-13 have been titled "Praise of the Shulamite's Beauty" (NKJV).

Voice: Verses 6:4-6 are seen as *his* words.

5. a. *Observe:* In 6:4-6, what are the most prominent metaphors and images?

_____

_____

_____

_____

b. What is each image being figuratively used to represent?

_____

_____

_____

_____

Optional Application: What are the images, ideas, and values in 6:1-3 that can have the most personal meaning for you in your own marriage?

For Thought and Discussion: What are the important factors for a couple to consider in finding the right balance between time together and time alone? Is it always true in a love relationship that absence makes the heart grow fonder?

97

Tirzah (6:4). City in northern Israel that for a time served as the residential city for the ruler of the northern kingdom (see 1 Kings 14:17). The bride's beauty is regal like this "renowned metropolis."[1]

Jerusalem (6:4). If it seems strange to compare a woman to a city, consider that the book of Revelation speaks of cities as women. There, Babylon is a prostitute and Jerusalem is the bride of Christ (see Revelation 18:2–19:3; 19:7-9; 21:1-2). We can imagine Christ speaking of His bride, the gathered people in His holy city.

Majestic (6:4). Literally, "awe-inspiring" or "terrifying." (Compare ESV "awesome" and KJV "terrible.")

6. a. *Respond and Reflect:* In 6:4-6, what qualities or values are being highlighted or suggested in each figurative comparison?

_____

_____

_____

_____

b. What do you find most evocative and delightful in the imagery you observed in this section?

_____

_____

_____

_____

7. Here in 6:4-6, in what ways, if any, do you see the following aspects of marital love reflected?

Giving of self: _____

_____

_____

Desire:_____

_____

_____

Delight in each other: _____

_____

_____

Commitment: _____

_____

_____

Marriage as a reflection of God's love: _____

_____

_____

_____

8. What creative title or heading would you suggest for this section?

_____

_____

_____

_____

6:7-9

Voice: Verses 6:7-9 are seen as *his* words.

9. a. *Observe:* In 6:7-9, what are the most prominent metaphors and images?

_____

_____

_____

_____

99

b. What is each image being figuratively used to represent?

_____

_____

_____

_____

My perfect one (6:9). She is perfect in his eyes. These are the words of a poet and a lover speaking from the heart, not the words of a moralist or scientist dissecting her to see if she is literally perfect in a provable way.

10. a. *Respond and Reflect:* In 6:7-9, what qualities or values are being highlighted or suggested in each figurative comparison?

_____

_____

_____

_____

b. What do you find most evocative and delightful in the imagery you observed in these lines?

_____

_____

_____

_____

11. Here in 6:7-9, in what ways, if any, do you see the following aspects of marital love reflected?

Giving of self: _____

_____

_____

Desire:_____

_____

_____

Delight in each other: _____

_____

_____

Commitment: _____

_____

_____

Marriage as a reflection of God's love: _____

_____

_____

_____

12. How do you see the man's description of the woman's body in 6:4-10 as a reflection of the creation doctrine that everything God made was "very good" (Genesis 1:31)?

_____

_____

_____

_____

13. What creative title or heading would you suggest for this section?

_____

_____

_____

_____

Optional Application: What are the images, ideas, and values in 6:7-9 that can have the most personal meaning for you in your own marriage?

6:10

Voice: Verse 6:10 is seen as either *his* words, or the words of *others*.

14. a. *Observe:* In 6:10, what are the most prominent metaphors and images?

_____

_____

_____

_____

b. What is each image being figuratively used to
represent?

_____

_____

_____

_____

15. a. *Respond and Reflect:* In 6:10, what qualities
or values are being highlighted or suggested
in each figurative comparison?

_____

_____

_____

_____

b. What do you find most evocative and delightful in the imagery you observed in this verse?

_____

_____

_____

_____

16. Here in 6:10, in what ways, if any, do you see
the following aspects of marital love reflected?

Giving of self: _____

_____

_____

Desire:_____

_____

_____

Delight in each other: _____

_____

_____

Commitment: _____

_____

_____

Marriage as a reflection of God's love: _____

_____

_____

_____

17. What creative title or heading would you suggest for this verse?

_____

_____

_____

_____

Optional Application: What are the images, ideas, and values in 6:10 that can have the most personal meaning for you in your own marriage?

6:11-12

Voice: Verses 6:11-12 are seen as either *her* words or *his* words. These verses comprise "a mysterious narrative fragment . . . ; it may be the woman's fantasy of what it is like to be with her beloved."[2]

18. a. *Observe:* In 6:11-12, what are the most prominent metaphors and images?

_____

_____

_____

_____

_____

b. What is each image being figuratively used to represent?

_____

_____

_____

_____

19. a. *Respond and Reflect:* In 6:11-12, what qualities or values are being highlighted or suggested in each figurative comparison?

_____

_____

_____

_____

b. What do you find most evocative and delightful in the imagery you observed in this section?

_____

_____

_____

_____

20. Here in 6:11-12, in what ways, if any, do you see the following aspects of marital love reflected?

Giving of self: _____

_____

_____

Desire:_____

_____

_____

Delight in each other: _____

_____

_____

Commitment: _____

_____

_____

Marriage as a reflection of God's love: _____

_____

_____

21. What creative title or heading would you suggest for this section?

_____

_____

_____

_____

6:13

Voice: Verse 6:13 is seen as the words of *others*, except for the question in the last line, which is seen as *his* words. Alternatively, the entire verse is seen as *his* words.

22. a. *Observe:* In 6:13, what are the most prominent metaphors and images?

_____

_____

_____

_____

Optional Application: What are the images, ideas, and values in 6:11-12 that can have the most personal meaning for you in your own marriage?

b. What is each image being figuratively used to represent?

_____

_____

_____

_____

Come back, come back (6:13). Possibly the bride and her husband have been temporarily separated, and she yearns for him again, so her friends call her to return. Or possibly this is still the husband speaking to his bride, who feels self-conscious, as if she is "performing a ritual dance in front of onlookers."[3]

Shulammite (6:13). Possibly a feminine variation of the name Solomon, which means "man of peace." Or it may be a variation of Shunammite, indicating that the woman is from Shunem, as was the "beautiful girl" who comforted David in his last days (see 1 Kings 1:3). Notice Solomon's involvement with that young woman in 1 Kings 2:13-21. See also 2 Kings 4:8-37 for the story of another woman from Shunem. It has also been suggested that "Shulammite" could be a variant of the feminine form of "Jerusalemite."[4]

---

23. a. *Respond and Reflect:* In 6:13, what qualities or values are being highlighted or suggested in each figurative comparison?

_____

_____

_____

b. What do you find most evocative and delightful in the imagery you observed in this verse?

_____

_____

_____

_____

Optional Application: What are the images, ideas, and values in 6:13 that can have the most personal meaning for you in your own marriage?

24. Here in 6:13, in what ways, if any, do you see the following aspects of marital love reflected?

Giving of self: _____

_____

_____

Desire:_____

_____

_____

Delight in each other: _____

_____

_____

Commitment: _____

_____

_____

Marriage as a reflection of God's love: _____

_____

_____

25. What creative title or heading would you suggest for this verse?

_____

_____

_____

_____

Optional Application: How has your study in chapter 6 of the Song of Solomon affected your perspective on the passion of married love?

Optional Application: Which passages in chapter 6 best reflect your own passion for your husband or wife and will be good to keep in mind?

Summary

26. What would you select as the key verse or passage in this portion of the Song—the lines that best capture or reflect the dynamics of what this section of the Song is all about?

_____

_____

_____

_____

27. List any lingering questions you have about chapter 6 in the Song of Solomon.

_____

_____

_____

_____

For the group

Again, you may want to focus your discussion especially on these concepts that are emphasized in the lesson's questions:

- The role of physical attractiveness in marriage
- Joys and tensions in marriage
- The meaning of marriage
- The joy of marital sex
- The permanence of married love

Remember to look also at the "For Thought and Discussion" question in the margin.

1. Ariel Bloch and Chana Bloch, *The Song of Songs: A New Translation with an Introduction and Commentary* (Berkeley: University of California Press, 1995), at Song 6:4.
2. Leland Ryken and Philip Graham Ryken, eds., *The Literary Study Bible* (Wheaton, IL: Crossway, 2007), at Song of Solomon 6:4.
3. Ryken and Ryken, *The Literary Study Bible*, at Song of Solomon 6:13.
4. Bloch and Bloch, *The Song of Songs*, at Song 7:1 [6:13 in English enumeration].

SONG OF SOLOMON 7

Further Enjoying

*I belong to my beloved,
and his desire is for me.*

SONG 7:10

7:1-3

Setting and Structure: Chapter 7 has been titled "Admiration by the Bridegroom" (NASB) and "The Wedding Dance" (CEV). Verses 7:1–8:4 have been titled "Expressions of Praise" (NKJV).

Voice: Verses 7:1-3 are seen as a continuation (from the last line in 6:13) of *his* words.

1. a. *Observe:* In 7:1-3, what are the most prominent metaphors and images?

   _____

   _____

   _____

   _____

   b. What is each image being figuratively used to represent?

   _____

_____

_____

_____

Your sandaled feet . . . your graceful legs (7:1).
Verse 6:13 referred to the woman dancing, and
now our gaze begins with her dancing feet and
moves upward to her head, the reverse of earlier
descriptions.

2. a. *Respond and Reflect:* In 7:1-3, what qualities
   or values are being highlighted or suggested
   in each figurative comparison?

   _____

   _____

   _____

   _____

   b. What do you find most evocative and delightful in the imagery you observed in these
   lines?

   _____

   _____

   _____

   _____

3. Here in 7:1-3, in what ways, if any, do you see
   the following aspects of marital love reflected?

   Giving of self: _____

   _____

   _____

   Desire:_____

   _____

   _____

Delight in each other: _____

_____

_____

Commitment: _____

_____

_____

Marriage as a reflection of God's love: _____

_____

_____

4. What creative title or heading would you suggest for this section?

_____

_____

_____

_____

_____

7:4-5

Voice: Verses 7:4-5 are seen as *his* words.

5. a. *Observe:* In 7:4-5, what are the most prominent metaphors and images?

_____

_____

_____

_____

b. What is each image being figuratively used to represent?

_____

_____

Optional Application: What are the images, ideas, and values in 7:1-3 that can have the most personal meaning for you in your own marriage?

111

For Further Study:
Notice how Mount
Carmel (see 7:5) also
serves as a strong
image for the biblical
prophets in Jeremiah
50:19; Amos 1:2;
Nahum 1:4; Isaiah
33:9; 35:2.

**Optional
Application:** What
are the images, ideas,
and values in 7:4-5
that can have the
most personal mean-
ing for you in your
own marriage?

Heshbon (7:4). "[T]he thriving capital of a once-
powerful neighboring state. . . . Heshbon was
famous for its great fertility and rich vineyards.
. . . It was well supplied with water, and remains
of a huge reservoir of excellent masonry have
recently been excavated on the site." [1]

Pools of Heshbon (7:4). These "are not natural
reservoirs, rather they are deep cisterns hewn
out of solid rock. The images conjured up here
are those of calmness, stillness, tranquility,
profundity." [2]

Bath Rabbim (7:4). "Presumably the name of the
gate of the city of Heshbon nearest the cisterns. . . . *Bath Rabbim* means 'daughter of
many' or 'daughter of noble people.'" [3]

Carmel (7:5). Her head is "as majestic as the huge
promontory of Mount Carmel, jutting out by
the Mediterranean Sea." [4]

6. a. *Respond and Reflect:* In 7:4-5, what qualities
or values are being highlighted or suggested
in each figurative comparison?

b. What do you find most evocative and delightful in the imagery you observed in this
section?

7. Here in 7:4-5, in what ways, if any, do you see the following aspects of marital love reflected?

Giving of self: _____

_____

_____

Desire: _____

_____

_____

Delight in each other: _____

_____

_____

Commitment: _____

_____

_____

Marriage as a reflection of God's love: _____

_____

_____

_____

8. What creative title or heading would you suggest for this section?

_____

_____

_____

_____

7:6-9a

Voice: Verses 7:6-9a are seen as *his* words.

9. a. *Observe:* In 7:6-9a, what are the most prominent metaphors and images?

_____

_____

_____

_____

   b. What is each image being figuratively used to represent?

_____

_____

_____

_____

10. a. *Respond and Reflect:* In 7:6-9a, what qualities or values are being highlighted or suggested in each figurative comparison?

_____

_____

_____

_____

   b. What do you find most evocative and delightful in the imagery you observed in these lines?

_____

_____

_____

_____

11. Here in 7:6-9a, in what ways, if any, do you see the following aspects of marital love reflected?

   Giving of self: _____

_____

_____

Desire:_____

_____

_____

Delight in each other: _____

_____

_____

Commitment: _____

_____

_____

Marriage as a reflection of God's love: _____

_____

_____

12. How do you see the man's description of the woman's body in 7:1-9a as a reflection of the creation doctrine that everything God made was "very good" (Genesis 1:31)?

_____

_____

_____

_____

13. What creative title or heading would you suggest for this section?

_____

_____

_____

_____

Optional Application: What are the images, ideas, and values in 7:6-9a that can have the most personal meaning for you in your own marriage?

7:9b-10

Setting and Structure: Verses 7:10–8:4 have been titled "The Bride's Tender Appeal."[6]

Voice: Verses 7:9b-10 are seen as *her* words.

14. a. *Observe:* In 7:9b-10, what are the most prominent metaphors and images?

_____

_____

_____

_____

  b. What is each image being figuratively used to represent?

_____

116

_____

_____

_____

I belong to my beloved (7:10). Compare this verse to 2:16 and 6:3. The mutuality of "and he is mine" is still true, but the self-abandonment is stronger here.

Desire (7:10). The only three uses in Scripture of this particular Hebrew noun are here and in the Cain and Abel story in Genesis 3:16 and 4:7.

15. a. *Respond and Reflect:* In 7:9b-10, what qualities or values are being highlighted or suggested in each figurative comparison?

_____

_____

_____

_____

   b. What do you find most evocative and delightful in the imagery you observed in this section?

_____

_____

_____

_____

16. Here in 7:9b-10, in what ways, if any, do you see the following aspects of marital love reflected?

   Giving of self: _____

_____

_____

   Desire: _____

_____

Delight in each other: _____

_____

_____

Commitment: _____

_____

_____

Marriage as a reflection of God's love: _____

_____

_____

_____

17. What creative title or heading would you suggest for this section?

_____

_____

_____

7:11-13

Setting and Structure: Verses 7:11-13 have been titled "The Bride Gives Her Love" (ESV).

Voice: Verses 7:11-13 are seen as *her* words.

18. a. *Observe:* In 7:11-13, what are the most prominent metaphors and images?

_____

_____

_____

_____

b. What is each image being figuratively used to represent?

118

_____

_____

_____

_____

19. a. *Respond and Reflect:* In 7:11-13, what qualities or values are being highlighted or suggested in each figurative comparison?

_____

_____

_____

_____

b. What do you find most evocative and delightful in the imagery you observed in these
lines?

_____

_____

_____

_____

Stored up for you (7:13). "The joys the two now are
experiencing in each other are but the beginning of raptures that she is prepared to bring to
him."[7]

20. Here in 7:11-13, in what ways, if any, do you see
the following aspects of marital love reflected?

Giving of self: _____

_____

_____

Desire:_____

_____

Optional Application: What are the images, ideas, and values in 7:11-13 that can have the most personal meaning for you in your own marriage?

Optional Application: Like the young man viewing his bride as "my perfect one" and "unique" (6:9), what are the important ways in which it's right for you to perceive the perfection and uniqueness of your husband or wife?

Optional Application: How has your study in chapter 7 of the Song of Solomon affected your perspective on the passion of married love?

Optional Application: Which passages in chapter 7 best reflect your own passion for your husband or wife and will be good to keep in mind?

Delight in each other: _____

_____

_____

Commitment: _____

_____

_____

Marriage as a reflection of God's love: _____

_____

_____

21. What creative title or heading would you suggest for this section?

_____

_____

_____

_____

Summary

22. What would you select as the key verse or passage in chapter 7 of the Song—the lines that best capture or reflect the dynamics of what this section of the Song is all about?

_____

_____

_____

_____

23. List any lingering questions you have about chapter 7 in the Song of Solomon.

_____

_____

120

For the group

Again, you may want to focus your discussion especially on these concepts that are emphasized in the lesson's questions:

- The role of physical attractiveness in marriage
- Joys and tensions in marriage
- The meaning of marriage
- The joy of marital sex
- The permanence of married love

1. Ariel Bloch and Chana Bloch, *The Song of Songs: A New Translation with an Introduction and Commentary* (Berkeley: University of California Press, 1995), at Song 7:4.
2. Tom Gledhill, *The Message of the Song of Songs*, The Bible Speaks Today (Downers Grove, IL: InterVarsity, 1994), 206–207.
3. Gledhill, *Song of Songs*, 207.
4. Gledhill, *Song of Songs*, 207.
5. M. Basil Pennington, *The Song of Songs: A Spiritual Commentary* (Woodstock, VT: SkyLight Paths, 2004), 69.
6. *Life Application Bible* (Wheaton, IL: Tyndale, 1990).
7. Dennis F. Kinlaw, "Song of Songs," in *Psalms, Proverbs, Ecclesiastes, Song of Songs*, Expositor's Bible Commentary, vol. 5, ed. Frank E. Gabelein (Grand Rapids, MI: Zondervan, 1990), 1239.

SONG OF SOLOMON 8

Expressing

> *Many waters cannot quench love;*
> *rivers cannot sweep it away.*
>
> SONG 8:7

8:1-2

Setting and Structure: Verses 8:1-7 have been titled "Longing for Her Beloved" (ESV). Chapter 8 has been titled "The Lovers Speak" (NASB) and "If Only You and I . . ." (CEV).

Voice: Verses 8:1-2 are seen as *her* words.

1. a. *Observe:* In 8:1-2, what are the most prominent metaphors and images?

   _____

   _____

   _____

   _____

   b. What is each image being figuratively used to represent?

   _____

   _____

_____

_____

Like a brother (8:1). The only man she could kiss in public would be a brother. If she kissed her lover, she would be treated as a shameful woman or even a prostitute. In Proverbs 7:10, a prostitute "with crafty intent" kisses a man in the street, and this is considered outrageous.

2. a. *Respond and Reflect:* In 8:1-2, what qualities or values are being highlighted or suggested in each figurative comparison?

_____

_____

_____

_____

   b. What do you find most evocative and delightful in the imagery you observed in this section?

_____

_____

_____

_____

"We end the Song of Solomon where we began it — with the couple falling in love all over again."[1]

3. Here in 8:1-2, in what ways, if any, do you see the following aspects of marital love reflected?

   Giving of self: _____

_____

_____

124

Desire:_____

_____

_____

Delight in each other: _____

_____

_____

Commitment: _____

_____

_____

Marriage as a reflection of God's love: _____

_____

_____

_____

4. What creative title or heading would you suggest for this section?

_____

_____

_____

_____

8:3-4

Voice: Verses 8:3-4 are seen as *her* words.

5. a. *Observe:* In 8:3-4, what are the most prominent metaphors and images?

_____

_____

_____

_____

Optional Application: What are the images, ideas, and values in 8:1-2 that can have the most personal meaning for you in your own marriage?

b. What is each image being figuratively used to represent?

_____

_____

_____

_____

His left arm . . . his right arm (8:3). Recall the first occurrence of this phrase in 2:6. "It seems that in the first instance the woman has been speaking about the man, perhaps in his absence, while in the second she has been speaking directly to him. But in both cases the verse following, which is a warning, is addressed to the Jerusalem girls."[2]

6. a. *Respond and Reflect:* In 8:3-4, what qualities or values are being highlighted or suggested in each figurative comparison?

_____

_____

_____

_____

b. What do you find most evocative and delightful in the imagery you observed in these lines?

_____

_____

_____

_____

7. Here in 8:3-4, in what ways, if any, do you see the following aspects of marital love reflected?

Giving of self: _____

_____

Desire: _____

_____

_____

Delight in each other: _____

_____

_____

Commitment: _____

_____

_____

Marriage as a reflection of God's love: _____

_____

_____

_____

8. What creative title or heading would you suggest for this section?

_____

_____

_____

_____

8:5-7

Setting and Structure: Verses 8:5-14 have been titled "Love Renewed in Lebanon" (NKJV) and "The Power of Love."[3]

Voice: Verses 8:5-7 are seen as *her* words, although verse 8:5 is also seen as the words of *others*.

9. a. *Observe:* In 8:5-7, what are the most prominent metaphors and images?

Optional Application: What are the images, ideas, and values in 8:3-4 that can have the most personal meaning for you in your own marriage?

Optional Application: In your marriage, how important is sexual satisfaction to your husband or wife? How important is it to you? How aware is your spouse of its importance to you?

**Optional
Application:** What
are the images, ideas,
and values in 8:5-7
that can have the
most personal mean-
ing for you in your
own marriage?

_____

_____

_____

_____

b. What is each image being figuratively used to
represent?

_____

_____

_____

_____

10. a. *Respond and Reflect:* In 8:5-7, what qualities
or values are being highlighted or suggested
in each figurative comparison?

_____

_____

_____

b. What do you find most evocative and delightful in the imagery you observed in this
section?

_____

_____

_____

_____

Who is this . . . leaning on her beloved? (8:5).
"There is a sense of fulfillment . . . when the
lovers, together at last and at ease in public,
walk arm-in-arm to the home of the parents,
the place where their relationship began."[4]

There your mother . . . gave you birth (8:5).
Many ancient myths depict a hero born under

a tree. This image makes the man seem to be a mythic hero.[5]

Like a seal over your heart, like a seal on your arm (8:6). Ancient Israelites carried a personal seal on a string around their neck or arm. The seal could be stamped in wax to function like a legal signature in a transaction such as a purchase. The bride wants her lover to claim her as his own and to keep her intimately near him. This verse may also echo Deuteronomy 11:18, which commands the Israelites to bind God's words onto their hands and foreheads, to hold them that close.

Death . . . grave . . . many waters (8:6-7). From the intimacy of heart and arm, the poet moves to the cosmic level: death, the underworld, and the "primordial waters"[6] that God separated when He created the world (see Genesis 1:6-8). Love is a "cosmic force" that can't be bought with wealth.

Many waters cannot quench love (8:7). This is especially true of Christ's love.

If one were to give all the wealth of one's house for love, it would be utterly scorned (8:7). Love is a supreme relational experience that is worlds apart from a commercial transaction. Those who try to buy love with any form of wealth, manipulation, performance, extortion, or flattery will be utterly scorned.

For Further Study:
Compare 8:6-7 with Isaiah 43:2. What connections do you see?

Stronger than Death

In 8:6-7, the love that was deeply of the body in earlier poems now transcends the body. Here is a wedding vow that insists on monogamy, that tolerates no other lovers. Committed human love is as strong as death, and divine love is stronger still — it triumphs over death and cleaves to the beloved with a holy jealousy. This love cannot be bought; it can only be given freely. Its fire cannot be quenched even if all the waters of creation flood over it.

(continued on page 130)

(continued from page 129)

This love may frighten us with its fierceness — do we dare get close to a love like that? Will we bind ourselves to this Lover's arm, to His heart? Will we let Him keep us close like a seal hung around His neck? Or will we shy away, preferring something less passionate, less demanding, more cerebral or sentimental?

11. Here in 8:5-7, in what ways, if any, do you see the following aspects of marital love reflected?

Giving of self: _____

_____

_____

Desire: _____

_____

_____

Delight in each other: _____

_____

_____

Commitment: _____

_____

_____

Marriage as a reflection of God's love: _____

_____

_____

_____

12. What creative title or heading would you suggest for this section?

_____

_____

_____

_____

13. In what ways do you see 8:6-7 as a summary climax to the Song?

_____

_____

_____

_____

For Further Study:
What connection to the message and theme of Song of Solomon do you see in these familiar passages about love: John 13:34-35; 15:17; Romans 12:9-10; 13:8; 1 Corinthians 13; 16:14; Galatians 5:13,22; 1 Timothy 1:5; 1 Peter 4:8; 1 John 4:7-8?

8:8-9

Setting and Structure: Verses 8:8-14 have been titled "Final Advice" (ESV).

Voice: Verses 8:8-9 are seen as the words of *others*, in particular the brothers of the bride.

14. a. *Observe:* In 8:8-9, what are the most prominent metaphors and images?

_____

_____

_____

_____

b. What is each image being figuratively used to represent?

_____

_____

_____

_____

_____

We will enclose her (8:9). The brothers affirm their opposition to their sister's marriage. In discussing love, the poet is realistic not just about the power of erotic desire but also about the

131

influence of interfering relatives. Most of the poems are set in an Eden-like fantasy world, but the poet knows we don't live in Eden. We live in a fallen world where family may be hostile to lovers. Still, he doesn't stop believing in the beauty, goodness, and satisfaction of human love.

15. a. *Respond and Reflect:* In 8:8-9, what qualities or values are being highlighted or suggested in each figurative comparison?

_____

_____

_____

_____

b. What do you find most evocative and delightful in the imagery you observed in these lines?

_____

_____

_____

_____

16. Here in 8:8-9, in what ways, if any, do you see the following aspects of marital love reflected?

Giving of self: _____

_____

_____

Desire:_____

_____

_____

Delight in each other: _____

_____

_____

Commitment: _____

_____

_____

Marriage as a reflection of God's love: _____

_____

_____

17. What creative title or heading would you suggest for this section?

_____

_____

_____

_____

Optional Application: What are the images, ideas, and values in 8:8-9 that can have the most personal meaning for you in your own marriage?

For Thought and Discussion: Do you find any significance in the fact that this Song about married love does not mention the procreation of children?

8:10-12

Voice: Verses 8:10-12 are seen as *her* words; alternatively, verses 8:11-12 are viewed as *his* words.

18. a. *Observe:* In 8:10-12, what are the most prominent metaphors and images?

_____

_____

_____

_____

b. What is each image being figuratively used to represent?

_____

_____

_____

_____

I am a wall (8:10). In 4:12 the woman was called a locked garden. Here she calls herself a wall, something that keeps her sexuality inaccessible behind a barrier. Her sexuality is all the more desirable for being hidden, guarded for the proper time and person.

19. a. *Respond and Reflect:* In 8:10-12, what qualities or values are being highlighted or suggested in each figurative comparison?

   _____

   _____

   _____

   _____

   _____

   b. What do you find most evocative and delightful in the imagery you observed in this section?

   _____

   _____

   _____

   _____

   _____

Solomon had a vineyard (8:11). Verses 8:11-12 compare the man to Solomon, and it turns out that the man has something even more valuable than Solomon's vineyard. The woman's vineyard, her womanhood, is something truly precious.

Baal Hamon (8:11). The name means "lord of great wealth." The poet may have invented this place name to allude to King Solomon.

Thousand shekels (8:11). In Isaiah 7:23, a vineyard that brings in a thousand silver shekels is a very valuable vineyard.

My own vineyard is mine (8:12). If the woman is speaking, then "my own vineyard" refers to her womanhood, which she chooses to give to the man to enjoy. If the man is speaking, then he is speaking of his bride in her fullness, whose fruit is now his to enjoy.

For you, Solomon (8:12). The meaning is, "Enjoy your thousand, O king—mine is better."

Optional Application: What are the images, ideas, and values in 8:10-12 that can have the most personal meaning for you in your own marriage?

20. Here in 8:10-12, in what ways, if any, do you see the following aspects of marital love reflected?

    Giving of self: _____

    _____

    _____

    Desire: _____

    _____

    _____

    Delight in each other: _____

    _____

    _____

    Commitment: _____

    _____

    _____

    Marriage as a reflection of God's love: _____

    _____

    _____

    _____

21. What creative title or heading would you suggest for this section?

    _____

    _____

135

_____

_____

8:13-14

Voice: In these closing lines, verse 8:13 is seen as *his* words, while verse 8:14 is seen as *her* words.

22. a. *Observe:* In 8:13-14, what are the most prominent metaphors and images?

_____

_____

_____

_____

   b. What is each image being figuratively used to represent?

_____

_____

_____

_____

You who dwell in the gardens (8:13). The poet has repeatedly likened the woman's body to a landscape: a vineyard, a locked garden. Appropriately, we see her for the last time sitting in a garden.

23. a. *Respond and Reflect:* In 8:13-14, what qualities or values are being highlighted or suggested in each figurative comparison?

_____

_____

_____

_____

b. What do you find most evocative and delightful in the imagery you observed in these
lines?

_____

_____

_____

_____

Come away (8:14). Or "make haste" (ESV); "hurry"
(NASB). The Hebrew word is normally translated
as "flee." Usually, one flees *from* something.
Here, the woman may be asking her lover to
flee *with* her. Or she may be urging him to flee
like a stag before the sun rises so that they
won't be caught together, as in 2:17. If the lat-
ter interpretation is right, then the poem ends
with them parting at dawn, an ending that
looks forward to their meeting again.

The woman calls, "Come away, my
beloved . . ." (8:14). The book of Revelation
tells us, "The Spirit and the bride say,
'Come!'" (Revelation 22:17). The bride
of Christ longs for Him to come, prays
for Him to come. He, too, invites her to
come. Love calls to love. "Amen. Come,
Lord Jesus" (Revelation 22:20).

24. Here in 8:13-14, in what ways, if any, do you see
the following aspects of marital love reflected?

Giving of self: _____

_____

_____

Desire:_____

_____

_____

Delight in each other: _____

_____

_____

Commitment: _____

_____

_____

Marriage as a reflection of God's love: _____

_____

_____

_____

25. What creative title or heading would you suggest for this section?

_____

_____

_____

_____

The Song doesn't arrive at a conclusion, as if "happily ever after" were the end of the story. The lovers' life together is just beginning. It will ebb and flow with the seasons. Sometimes the man will call out for his beloved's voice and have to wait for a response. Sometimes they will be parted, taking separate paths for a time. "But there is always the coming back and starting anew, the making of fresh beginnings."[7] Though their lives go through cycles, their commitment is secure. Each cycle will bring renewed depth to their intimacy.

Summary

26. What would you select as the key verse or passage in chapter 8 — the lines that best capture or reflect the dynamics of what this final portion of the Song is all about?

_____

_____

_____

_____

27. List any lingering questions you have about this final chapter in the Song of Solomon.

_____

_____

_____

_____

_____

Reviewing the Song of Solomon

28. In your study of the Song of Solomon, what has God brought most to your attention regarding each of these aspects of marital love?

Giving of self: _____

_____

_____

Desire:_____

_____

For Further Study: Read Proverbs 30:18-19, especially the last line of the passage. How is that line more fully reflected in the Song of Solomon?

Optional Application: How has your study of chapter 8 of the Song of Solomon affected your perspective on the passion of married love?

Optional Application: Which passages in chapter 8 best reflect your own passion for your husband or wife and will be good to keep in mind?

For Thought and Discussion: What is the best evidence you've seen in the Song of Solomon that the passion of married love is both *good* and *enjoyable*?

Optional Application: From your study of the Song of Solomon, what has been most helpful for your life and marriage?

Delight in each other: _____

_____

_____

Commitment: _____

_____

_____

Marriage as a reflection of God's love: _____

_____

_____

_____

29. In Isaiah 55:10-11, God reminds us that in the same way He sends rain and snow from the sky to water the earth and nurture life, so also He sends His words to accomplish specific purposes. What would you suggest are God's primary purposes for the message of the Song of Solomon in the lives of His people today?

_____

_____

_____

_____

30. Recall the guidelines given for our thought life in Philippians 4:8 — "Whatever is true, whatever is noble, whatever is right, whatever is pure, whatever is lovely, whatever is admirable — if anything is excellent or praiseworthy — *think about such things*" (emphasis added). As you reflect on all you've read in the Song of Solomon, what stands out to you as being particularly *true*, or *noble*, or *right*, or *pure*, or *lovely*, or *admirable*, or *excellent*, or *praiseworthy* — and therefore well worth thinking more about?

_____

_____

_____

_____

Will We Follow?

What makes this the Song above all songs? It speaks to our deepest longings. The longing for love, for that one person with whom we can share ourselves utterly, body and soul. The longing for passion, for something more than a flat, safe life. The longing for delight, for the full satisfaction of our senses without degrading ourselves or others. The longing for Eden, for a world rich and beautiful to be savored. And because we know this life offers only tastes of the fulfillment of these longings, the Song points beyond itself to the Lover who truly satisfies. Love, passion, delight, paradise — if we seek these in Him, we will find what we long for. The tastes here and now are promises as our Lover runs ahead of us like a stag on the spice-laden mountains. Will we follow?

For Thought and Discussion: As we looked at in the first lesson, throughout Scripture we see God using marriage as a picture of His own love relationship with His people, and of Christ's love relationship with the church. Now that you've studied through all of the Song of Solomon, in what appropriate ways might we apply the images and themes in the Song to the Lord's relationship with us?

31. Since all of Scripture testifies ultimately of Christ, in what way, if any, does *Jesus* come more into focus for you in this book?

_____

_____

_____

32. In your understanding, is there any way in which the Song of Solomon points us to mankind's need for Jesus and what He accomplished in His death and resurrection?

_____

_____

_____

_____

141

33. In Romans 15:4, Paul reminds us that the Old Testament Scriptures can give us patience and perseverance on one hand, as well as comfort and encouragement on the other. In your own life and marriage, how do you see the Song of Solomon living up to Paul's description? In what ways does it help to meet your personal needs in marriage for both *perseverance* and *encouragement*?

_____

_____

_____

_____

For the group

Once more, you may want to focus your discussion especially on these concepts that are emphasized in the lesson's questions:

- The role of physical attractiveness in marriage
- Joys and tensions in marriage
- The meaning of marriage
- The joy of marital sex
- The permanence of married love

Allow enough discussion time to look back together and review all of the Song of Solomon as a whole. You can use the numbered questions 28–33 in this lesson to help you do that.

Once more, look also at the questions in the margins under the heading "For Thought and Discussion."

1. Leland Ryken and Philip Graham Ryken, eds., *The Literary Study Bible* (Wheaton, IL: Crossway, 2007), at Song of Solomon 8:1.
2. Elizabeth Huwiler, "Song of Songs," in *Proverbs, Ecclesiastes, Song of Songs*, by Roland E. Murphy and Elizabeth Huwiler, New International Biblical Commentary (Peabody, MA: Hendrickson, 1999), 227.
3. *Life Application Bible* (Wheaton, IL: Tyndale, 1990).
4. *New Geneva Study Bible* (Nashville: Nelson, 1995), introduction to Song of Solomon: "Characteristics and Themes."
5. Ariel Bloch and Chana Bloch, *The Song of Songs: A New Translation with an Introduction and Commentary*

(Berkley: University of California Press, 1995), at Song 8:5.

6. Robert Alter, afterword to *The Song of Songs* by Bloch and Bloch, 131.

7. Tom Gledhill, *The Message of the Song of Songs*, The Bible Speaks Today (Downers Grove, IL: InterVarsity, 1994), 234.

STUDY AIDS

Some well-received commentaries on the Song of Solomon

G. Lloyd Carr, *The Song of Solomon: An Introduction and Commentary* (Tyndale Old Testament Commentary, InterVarsity, 1984).

Franz Delitzsch, *Commentary on the Song of Songs and Ecclesiastes*, translated by M. G. Easton (Biblical Commentary on the Old Testament, by C. F. Keil and F. Delitzsch, Eerdmans, 1950).

Tom Gledhill, *The Message of the Song of Songs: The Lyrics of Love* (The Bible Speaks Today, InterVarsity, 1994).

Richard S. Hess, *Song of Songs* (Baker Commentary on the Old Testament Wisdom and Psalms, Baker, 2005).

David A. Hubbard, *Ecclesiastes, Song of Solomon* (Mastering the Old Testament, Word, 1991).

Othmar Keel, *The Song of Songs*, translated by Frederick J. Gaiser (Continental Commentary, Fortress, 1994).

Tremper Longman III, *Song of Songs* (New International Commentary on the Old Testament, Eerdmans, 2001).

Roland E. Murphy, *The Song of Songs* (Hermeneia, Fortress, 1990).

Marvin H. Pope, *Song of Songs* (The Anchor Bible, Doubleday, 1977).

Iain Provan, *Ecclesiastes, Song of Songs* (NIV Application Commentary, Zondervan, 2001).

Other good study tools: a sampling

The New Bible Dictionary, edited by I. Howard Marshall, A. R. Millard, J. I. Packer, and D. J. Wiseman (InterVarsity, 1996).

The New Unger's Bible Dictionary, edited by Merrill F. Unger, R. K. Harrison, Howard F. Vos, and Cyril J. Barber (Moody, 2006).

Zondervan Encyclopedia of the Bible, revised edition, edited by Merrill C. Tenney and Moisés Silva (Zondervan, 2009).

Zondervan Handbook to the Bible, David and Pat Alexander (Zondervan, 2002).

MacArthur Bible Handbook, John MacArthur (Nelson, 2003).

Nelson's Compact Bible Handbook, edited by George Knight and James Edwards (Nelson, 2004).

The Bible Almanac, edited by J. I. Packer, Merrill C. Tenney, and William White Jr. (Nelson, 1980).

Historical background sources and handbooks

Bible study becomes more meaningful when modern Western readers understand the times and places in which the biblical authors lived. *The IVP Bible Background Commentary: Old Testament*, by John H. Walton, Victor H. Matthews, and Mark Chavalas (InterVarsity, 2000), provides insight into the ancient Near Eastern world, its peoples, customs, and geography to help contemporary readers better understand the context in which the Old Testament Scriptures were written.

A **handbook** of biblical customs can also be useful. Some good ones are the time-proven updated classic *Halley's Bible Handbook with the New International Version*, by Henry H. Halley (Zondervan, 2007), and the inexpensive paperback *Manners and Customs in the Bible*, by Victor H. Matthews (Hendrickson, 1991).

Concordances, dictionaries, and encyclopedias

A **concordance** lists words of the Bible alphabetically along with each verse in which the word appears. It lets you do your own word studies. An *exhaustive* concordance lists every word used in a given translation, while an *abridged* or *complete* concordance omits either some words, some occurrences of the word, or both.

Two of the best exhaustive concordances are *Strong's Exhaustive Concordance* and *The Strongest NIV Exhaustive Concordance*. *Strong's* is available based on the King James Version of the Bible and the New American Standard Bible. *Strong's* has an index by which you can find out which Greek or Hebrew word is used in a given English verse. The NIV concordance does the same thing except it also includes an index for Aramaic words in the original texts from which the NIV was translated. However, neither concordance requires knowledge of the original languages. *Strong's* is available online at www.biblestudytools.com. Both are also available in hard copy.

A **Bible dictionary** or **Bible encyclopedia** alphabetically lists articles about people, places, doctrines, important words, customs, and geography of the Bible.

Holman Illustrated Bible Dictionary, by C. Brand, C. W. Draper, and A. England (B&H, 2003), offers more than seven hundred color photos, illustrations, and charts; sixty full-color maps; and up-to-date archeological findings, along with exhaustive definitions of people, places, things, and events—dealing with every subject in the Bible. It uses a variety of Bible translations and is the only dictionary that includes the HCSB, NIV, KJV, RSV, NRSV, REB, NASB, ESV, and TEV.

The New Unger's Bible Dictionary, Revised and Expanded, by Merrill F. Unger (Moody, 2006), has been a best seller for almost fifty years. Its 6,700-plus entries reflect the most current scholarship and more than 1,200,000 words are supplemented with detailed essays, colorful photography and maps, and dozens of charts and illustrations to enhance your understanding of God's Word. Based on the New American Standard Version.

The Zondervan Encyclopedia of the Bible, edited by Moisés Silva and Merrill C. Tenney (Zondervan, 2008), is excellent and exhaustive. However, its five 1,000-page volumes are a financial investment, so all but very serious students may prefer to use it at a church, public college, or seminary library.

Unlike a Bible dictionary in the above sense, *Vine's Complete Expository Dictionary of Old and New Testament Words*, by W. E. Vine, Merrill F. Unger, and William White Jr. (Thomas Nelson, 1996), alphabetically lists major words used in the King James Version and defines each Old Testament Hebrew or New Testament Greek word the KJV translates with that English word. *Vine's* lists verse references where that Hebrew or Greek word appears so that you can do your own cross-references and word studies without knowing the original languages.

The Brown-Driver-Briggs Hebrew and English Lexicon, by Francis Brown, C. Briggs, and S. R. Driver (Hendrickson, 1996), is probably the most respected and comprehensive Bible lexicon for Old Testament studies. *BDB* gives not only dictionary definitions for each word but relates each word to its Old Testament usage and categorizes its nuances of meaning.

Bible atlases and map books

A **Bible atlas** can be a great aid to understanding what is going on in a book of the Bible and how geography affected events. Here are a few good choices:

The Hammond Atlas of Bible Lands (Langenscheidt, 2007) packs a ton of resources into just sixty-four pages. Maps, of course, but also photographs, illustrations, and a comprehensive timeline. Includes an introduction to the unique geography of the Holy Land, including terrain, trade routes, vegetation, and climate information.

The New Moody Atlas of the Bible, by Barry J. Beitzel (Moody, 2009), is scholarly, very evangelical, and full of theological text, indexes, and references. Beitzel shows vividly how God prepared the land of Israel perfectly for the acts of salvation He was going to accomplish in it.

Then and Now Bible Maps Insert (Rose, 2008) is a nifty paperback that is sized just right to fit inside your Bible cover. Only forty-four pages long, it features clear plastic overlays of modern-day cities and countries so you can see what nation or city now occupies the Bible setting you are reading about. Every major city of the Bible is included.

For small-group leaders

Discipleship Journal's Best Small-Group Ideas, Volumes 1 and 2 (NavPress, 2005). Each volume is packed with 101 of the best hands-on tips and group-building principles from *Discipleship Journal's* "Small Group Letter" and "DJ Plus" as well as articles from the magazine. They will help you inject new passion into the life of your small group.

Donahue, Bill. *Leading Life-Changing Small Groups* (Zondervan, 2002). This comprehensive resource is packed with information, practical tips, and insights that will teach you about small-group philosophy and structure, discipleship, conducting meetings, and more.

McBride, Neal F. *How to Build a Small-Groups Ministry* (NavPress, 1994). *How to Build a Small-Groups Ministry* is a time-proven, hands-on workbook for pastors and lay leaders that includes everything you need to know to develop a plan that fits your unique church. Through basic principles, case studies, and worksheets, McBride leads you through twelve logical steps for organizing and administering a small-groups ministry.

McBride, Neal F. *How to Lead Small Groups* (NavPress, 1990). This book covers leadership skills for all kinds of small groups: Bible study, fellowship, task, and support groups. Filled with step-by-step guidance and practical exercises to help you grasp the critical aspects of small-group leadership and dynamics.

Miller, Tara, and Jenn Peppers. *Finding the Flow: A Guide for Leading Small Groups and Gatherings* (IVP Connect, 2008). *Finding the Flow* offers a fresh take on leading small groups by seeking to develop the leader's small-group facilitation skills.

Bible study methods

Discipleship Journal's Best Bible Study Methods (NavPress, 2002). This is a collection of thirty-two creative ways to explore Scripture that will help you enjoy studying God's Word more.

Hendricks, Howard, and William Hendricks. *Living by the Book: The Art and Science of Reading the Bible* (Moody, 2007). *Living by the Book* offers a practical three-step process that will help you master simple yet effective inductive methods of observation, interpretation, and application that will make all the difference in your time with God's Word. A workbook by the same title is also available to go along with the book.

The Navigator Bible Studies Handbook (NavPress, 1994). This resource teaches the underlying principles for doing good inductive Bible study, including instructions on doing queston-and-answer studies, verse-analysis studies, chapter-analysis studies, and topical studies.

Warren, Rick. *Rick Warren's Bible Study Methods: Twelve Ways You Can Unlock God's Word* (HarperCollins, 2006). Rick Warren offers simple, step-by-step instructions, guiding you through twelve different approaches to studying the Bible for yourself with the goal of becoming more like Jesus.

Discover What the Bible Really Says

LIFECHANGE by The Navigators

The LIFECHANGE Bible study series can help you grow in Christlikeness through a life-changing encounter with God's Word. Discover what the Bible says—not what someone else thinks it says—and develop the skills and desire to dig even deeper into God's Word. Each study includes study aids and discussion questions.

NAV ESSENTIALS

Voices of The Navigators—Past, Present, and Future

NavEssentials offer core Navigator messages from such authors as Jim Downing, LeRoy Eims, Mike Treneer, and more — at an affordable price. This new series will deeply influence generations in the movement of discipleship. Learn from the old and new messages of The Navigators how powerful and transformational the life of a disciple truly is.

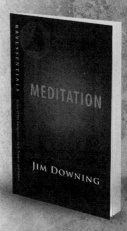  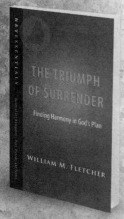

Meditation
by Jim Downing
9781615217250 | $5.00

Advancing the Gospel
by Mike Treneer
9781617471575 | $5.00

The Triumph of Surrender
by William M. Fletcher
9781615219070 | $5.00

Available wherever books are sold. NAVPRESS